HOUSE OF COMMONS LIBRARY

LOCATION	MI R331.2
AUTHOR	
Acc DATE	D0120247

2 4 AUG 82

HOUSE OF COMMONS LIBRARY

TO BE
DISPOSED
BY
AUTHORITY

House of Commons Library

54056001071262

A theory of inequality and taxation

A theory of
inequality and taxation

PATRICIA APPS

CAMBRIDGE UNIVERSITY PRESS

Cambridge
London   New York   New Rochelle
Melbourne   Sydney

Published by the Press Syndicate of the University of Cambridge
The Pitt Building, Trumpington Street, Cambridge CB2 1RP
32 East 57th Street, New York, NY 10022, USA
296 Beaconsfield Parade, Middle Park, Melbourne 3206, Australia

© Cambridge University Press 1981

First published 1981

Printed in Malta

British Library Cataloguing in Publication Data
Apps, Patricia
A theory of inequality and taxation.
1. Equality   2. Income distribution
– Great Britain   3. Great Britain – Economic
conditions – 1945–
I. Title
330.9′41′0857   HB821   81–3881
ISBN 0 521 23437 9

HOUSE OF COMMONS
LIBRARY
CATALOGUED

Contents

Preface

The theory of taxation has been built on a theory of inequality which attributes income differences to the natural abilities, inherited capital and the preferences of individuals. Differences in individual endowments caused by the structure of institutions are acknowledged but not given a fundamentally different treatment. Yet institutions play a central role in the creation of inequality and, as well, in its perpetuation, and the latter is not captured by conventional tax models.

This book presents a theory of institutional inequality which, in analysing taxation, employs a modified trade model and the theory of local public goods. The analysis shows that tax incidence depends upon the causes of inequality. If inequality is largely institutional and social policy does not alter the mechanisms by which institutions translate the distribution of power among individuals into the distribution of income, progressive taxation may be ineffective in reducing inequality and alleviating poverty. Under these conditions there is no trade-off between efficiency and equity in the design of tax reform.

The theory presented has evolved over a number of years and during this time I have benefitted greatly from access to work in progress by Elizabeth Savage on the treatment of resources in trade models. The exposition of Chapter 2 in particular has been influenced by her critique of general equilibrium tax incidence analysis. I am also grateful to Glenn Jones for access to his papers on optimal tax theory and for the opportunity of working with him on the development of optimal tax models which introduce additional institutional constraints on tax design.

I wish to thank Tony Atkinson for his detailed comments and suggestions which I found most helpful in redrafting the manuscript and Kerry Schott for her encouraging and guiding critique. An important acknowledgement is due to Martin Ravallion who read the manuscript in its early draft stage and offered constructive criticisms. I thank Nicholas Barr and Julian Le Grand for their comments on the work while I was an Academic Visitor at the London School of Economics.

Finally, I would like to thank Gary Aitchison who has read and commented extensively on the final draft. I am most grateful for the time and effort he has put into improving the book.

P. A.

June 1980

1

Introduction: the theory in outline

1.1 Tax theory and the causes of inequality

All taxes fall on the real incomes of individuals. The calculation of tax incidence becomes difficult when the individuals upon whom a tax is levied can switch to an activity which is untaxed or taxed at a lower rate. Those who formally pay the tax may shift at least part of the burden to others. To find the effective incidence of a tax or expenditure policy, as opposed to its formal incidence, involves the determination of equilibrium prices and incomes before and after a policy is introduced. Because general equilibrium studies of this kind are complex, much of the analysis of tax policy has been conducted within a partial equilibrium framework which depends on assumptions now widely criticised as unnecessarily restrictive. Emphasis in recent theory is placed on a general equilibrium approach to tax design and to the calculation of tax incidence and tax distortions. Two major directions of study can be identified.

One direction is that taken in optimal tax theory which seeks to derive rules for optimal tax design.[1] The Ramsey paper of 1927 on optimal indirect taxation showed how the partial equilibrium result that equi-proportional indirect taxation was optimal, held only under special conditions. Recent contributions, beginning with Mirrlees (1971) and Diamond and Mirrlees (1971), extend the theory and derive rules for optimal tax design taking distributional considerations into account. A second direction is taken in the analysis of excise and factor taxes using the two-sector general equilibrium model of international trade theory. This development was initiated by the Harberger (1962) model of the factor distribution of the burden of a

1

tax on capital in the corporate sector. In subsequent studies the model has been used to determine the income distribution effects of factor payment differentials caused by unions and factor immobilities.[2] In contrast to optimal tax theory in which the individual is the unit of analysis,[3] this kind of model examines the effects of taxation on factors and, by implication, on classes or groups of individuals distinguished by their 'initial endowments' of labour and capital.

These developments encompass the present emphasis of tax theory. They represent applications of competitive general equilibrium theory and, despite some modifications, leave unchanged the underlying theory of inequality. In the optimal tax literature income inequality is attributed to differences in the initial endowments and tastes of individuals which are referred to as 'given characteristics'. In general equilibrium analyses of factor market distortions, the effects of institutional differentials in factor payments on individual endowments are not identified.[4] The models treat all factors as given endowments and introduce institutional inequality in a way which is analogous to introducing another kind of endowment.[5] Thus, institutional inequality is recognised but the relationship between individual ownership of capital and wage differentials is not adequately specified.

In both partial and general equilibrium models, individual consumers and producers behave as perfectly competitive agents, taking prices as given. This can be interpreted to mean that the initial endowments of consumers are not influenced by institutional controls exercised by more powerful agents only if all individuals act perfectly competitively in every period. Under this condition inequality cannot be attributed to restrictions imposed now or in the past by differential control of institutions by individuals. Individual endowments and tastes are given characteristics at the beginning of each and every production period. In this sense inequality is apolitical.

In an environment where the competitive equilibrium achieves a Pareto efficient allocation of resources but not necessarily an optimal distribution of income, a given characteristics theory of inequality implies that the optimal tax system is a very simple one, provided the characteristics are observable. The 'socially just' distribution of income can, in principle, be achieved by a suitable reallocation of initial endowments among consumers; that is, by lump sum taxes and transfers. For example, if individuals possess different innate abilities, lump sum taxes and transfers of appropriate amounts according to each individual's innate ability can provide a first best solution to the social welfare maximization problem. The tax-transfer scheme is non-distortionary because the innate ability of each individual is a characteristic which cannot be altered by switching from taxed to untaxed activity.

The problem in tax design is said to arise because individual endowments and tastes are not observable. Only indicators of endowments can be observed and although ideally governments would like to tax given characteristics, they are limited to taxing indicators which can be altered by the behaviour of individuals. In particular, innate ability cannot be observed and when wage income is taxed as an indicator of ability, the individual may reduce its labour supply to work by switching to leisure which is untaxed. Unless the elasticity of substitution between taxed work and untaxed leisure is zero, the tax is distortionary. While the tax may increase social welfare by reducing inequality, it is associated with an excess burden or welfare loss because of its distortionary effects. The central problem in tax design is seen in terms of the trade-off between the welfare gain from increased equality and the welfare loss caused by the differential taxation of activities.[6]

The theory of optimal taxation is held to overcome the objection that the minimum sacrifice theory failed to take account of the distortionary effects of income taxation.[7] The derivation of second best solutions to tax design when the untaxability of leisure imposes a single additional constraint on the maximization of social welfare is, however, a further development within the Edgeworth tradition which is built on the premise that inequality is apolitical. The optimal tax problem is thus formulated on the basis of the same apolitical theory of inequality implicit in the minimum sacrifice theory and the arguments for redistribution by Pigou (1922) and Simons (1938).

The premise that inequality is apolitical is questionable when it can be observed that there are differences in incomes caused by institutional restrictions on job choices and that institutions are under the control of society's more powerful individuals. Examples are differences between the wages for labour groups distinguished by non-economic characteristics of sex, colour and ethnic origin. Other examples are wage differentials between managerial positions, between managerial and non-managerial jobs and between professional and non professional occupations, where the differentials are maintained by entry quotas.

Theories of discrimination by Becker (1957), Arrow (1972) and others[8] explain wage differentials between labour groups in terms of a taste for discrimination. This approach can be seen as a variant of the given characteristics theory since it identifies an additional aspect of given tastes which can, like other characteristics, impose the binding constraint on supply necessary for a factor payment differential in a competitive market. In contrast, theories of labour market segmentation emphasise the role of institutional constraints on entry into higher wage jobs. Doeringer and Piore (1971, 1975), for example, suggest that there are two labour markets: an internal labour market (or primary sector), which is protected from competitive forces, and an external labour market (or secondary sector) which is not. Low wages characterise employment in the external labour market. In recognising institutional constraints on the demand side of the labour market, the theory departs from the neoclassical explanation of wage inequality. The job competition model posited by Thurow (1972, 1975) also attributes wage differentials to constraints on the demand side of the labour market.[9] Although contributions to the literature on institutional inequality emphasise that different policies are required under institutional constraints, tax theory remains firmly grounded upon an innate or inherited endowments theory of inequality.[10] The aim of the analysis here is to examine tax incidence and tax distortions taking account of the way in which institutional inequality is initiated and perpetuated. The proposed theory employs two kinds of models: a modified two sector international trade model and a local public goods model.

1.2 Institutional inequality

To focus on the implications of institutional inequality we can consider an economy where incomes are equal in the absence of institutional constraints. Individuals of the same age possess identical innate abilities and tastes.[11] Given characteristics vary only by age. When individuals are identical and production exhibits constant returns to scale throughout, there is no reason for trade or social interaction. To explain the formation of trading groups by identical individuals it is necessary to introduce scale economies. In the presence of scale economies the formation of trading groups involves the production of local public goods. From the theory of local public goods[12] we know that there can be inequality between groups formed by identical individuals if there are constraints on community size. To rule out inequality of this kind, we assume that population is variable in the absence of institutional constraints: that the necessary conditions exist for the formation of groups of optimal size. If there always exists a complete set of perfectly competitive markets, the competitive equilibrium is Pareto efficient and is associated with an equal distribution of income within and between local communities. If social justice is taken to mean the equal treatment of equals, the competitive equilibrium is also optimal.

Given such an equal and optimal society, we assume a random event introduces an unequal distribution of power. Thereafter, more powerful individuals impose binding restrictions on the mobility of less powerful individuals. The essential feature of 'power' as the term is used here is that it is not a productive endowment. Individuals with greater power derive higher incomes only by using their power to influence the law or social opinion so that these institutions impose binding restrictions on what others can do. Thus, an event which gives an individual greater power does not permanently affect the distribution of income unless it is used to distort the economy.[13] For example, males may once have had a physical strength wage advantage[14] which gave them the power to introduce social attitudes which impose constraints thereafter on the employment of females in occupations using skills other than strength.

The proposed theory of institutional inequality explores the extent to which segregation and inequality might be explained by constraints on mobility imposed by social institutions under the control of more powerful members of society. In presenting the theory particular reference is made to the following:

(i) restrictions on entry into higher wage market sector occupations and job positions;
(ii) restrictions on the entry of females into market sector occupations and job positions;

(iii) restrictions on the size of households; and
(iv) restrictions on a child's access to lifetime income according
to parent income,

where these restrictions are imposed by professional associations, by
management policy, by trade unions, by social attitudes and/or by
government policy.

Under constant returns to scale, binding constraints on entry into
trading sectors or occupations are required for inequality.[15] A theory
of institutional inequality under these conditions is presented in
Chapter 2. The model is a modified two sector trade model. There are
two key propositions. The first is that there are institutional restrictions on the number of individuals employed in each sector of the
economy. The introduction of the restrictions results in short run
changes in the composition of output, in relative prices and thus in
marginal value products of individual time in each sector. Although
individuals of the same age have innately identical productivities and
preferences, they receive different wages. A high wage is obtained from
employment in a 'crowding' occupation and a low wage from employment in a 'crowded' occupation.[16] The former refers to sectors in
which employment is reduced by entry restrictions and the latter to
sectors in which employment is increased. When restrictions (i) and (ii)
above are binding, crowded sectors include low wage market occupations and the household sector which includes the 'unemployed'
who, by definition, are limited to employment in the household sector.

The second proposition is that an individual's capital is also subject
to entry restrictions. Constant returns to scale production functions
are assumed to be circular (as in von Neumann (1945))[17] and individuals restricted to employment in crowded sectors invest their
savings in equally crowded sectors. This restriction on capital mobility
is easily seen for the special case of human capital which, in an
imperfect capital market, can be financed only from each individual's
savings (or parents' savings) from wage income. It is therefore a useful
example to illustrate the principle.

Individuals in crowded activities, since they have lower incomes for
purchasing investment goods in subsequent periods, develop fewer
skills than labour in high wage sectors. Consequently, output per unit
time in crowded sectors falls relative to the output in uncrowded

sectors, offsetting the short run price effects. Prices tend to return to pre-crowding prices. The economy may appear to function as if there is no crowding because, in the long run, there may be little change in the composition of output and in relative prices: it can appear efficient. However, although individuals may obtain near pre-crowding prices for their output, individuals in uncrowded sectors are producing more output and therefore receive higher wages. There are no longer differences in wage payments at the same productivity. High wage individuals appear to be innately more productive because institutional restrictions are considered unimportant. The high wage sectors are relatively capital-intensive and the low wage sectors time-intensive. The theory explains differences in factor intensities, in endowments and in incomes in terms of the distribution of power.

The theory offers an explanation for the perpetuation of inequality within each generation. Because an entry restriction imposed on the basis of a characteristic such as sex or colour produces productivity or ability differences the restriction can, in subsequent periods, be placed on indicators of ability with the same effect. When, in addition, access to income for children is tied to the income of parents, the model offers an explanation for the perpetuation of inequality from one generation to the next: induced productivity differences among parents are reproduced among children. Schooling screens for induced ability differences and so an initial restriction imposed on an arbitrary labour characteristic can be placed on ability as indicated by school grades or level of education, again with the same effect.

If entry restrictions must appear to be fair for long term political viability, they must be imposed on the basis of a labour characteristic which appears to justify exclusion from an occupation. When the characteristic most 'acceptable' as a criterion for limiting entry is ability, the repeated imposition of a restriction according to a characteristic which is uncorrelated with ability may not be politically sustainable. However, because ability becomes correlated with the characteristics used for screening, we have an economy in which crowding inequality can be perpetuated intergenerationally and made to appear the result of given individual characteristics. The inter-generational perpetuation of inequality in this way is discussed in Chapter 3.

A limitation of a theory of institutional inequality based on the premise that there are binding restrictions on entry into high wage sectors is that it offers an explanation for inequality only if the institutions can be observed to control the activities of crowded sectors. There must be evidence of regulation of the kinds of goods produced by low wage sectors, otherwise individuals facing restrictions on entry could form a separate economy. Although there are many instances where the production of services, such as professional services, is regulated, this is not always the case. For example, the household sector is not regulated to produce particular services.

To account for crowding when there is no explicit regulation of the activities of crowded sectors, it is proposed that in addition to restrictions on entry into high wage sectors within a trading community there are institutional restrictions on the formation of groups by individuals distinguished by arbitrary characteristics. Constraints on group or local community size can create inequality between groups. However, the inequality is not evidenced unless the groups trade, and so it is proposed that there are binding constraints on the size of groups which together form a trading sector of a larger trading community. The constraints control what the sector can produce and, thereby, the terms of trade. In Chapter 4 trade between the market and household sectors is examined in this context.

If inequality is due to institutional distortions, this raises questions concerning the relevance not only of the results of received tax theory but, as well, of debates on social justice and the choice of a social welfare function which presupposes apolitical inequality. For example, when inequality is institutional the Rawlsian[18] 'veil of ignorance' is ignorance about the distribution of power. There is inequality because the more powerful individuals in society choose the rules and institutions which constitute the social contract.

1.3 An illustration of institutional inequality

The analysis of taxation depends extensively on the application of the theory of institutional inequality presented in Chapter 2. To give an illustration of the principle involved we can consider how inequality might develop in the two sector economy described by Adam Smith.

In 1776 Smith wrote:

In that early rude state of society which precedes both the accumulation of stock and the appropriation of land, the proportion between the quantities of labour necessary for acquiring different objects seems to be the only circumstance which can afford any rule for exchanging them for one another. If among a nation of hunters, for example, it usually costs twice the labour time to kill a beaver which it does to kill a deer, one beaver should naturally exchange for or be worth two deer [p. 150].

and in contrast he observed:

As soon as stock has accumulated in the hands of particular persons, some of them will naturally employ it in setting to work industrious people, whom they will supply with materials and subsistence, in order to make a profit by the sale of their work, or by what their labour adds to the value of the materials [p. 151].

The difference between the two economies, however, does not depend on the level of accumulation.[19] It depends on the premise that the hunting economy has free entry and trade between identical individuals while the economy with 'stock' has restricted entry and trade between heterogeneous individuals.

The hunting economy could equally well exhibit inequality. Assume deer and beaver are imperfect substitutes and with free entry the two industries employ the same number of equally skilled hunters. Assume further that while all hunters are equally skilled, they comprise 50 per cent white labour and 50 per cent black labour, each of which is 50 per cent male and 50 per cent female. Let us suppose that political conditions develop which exclude the entry of black labour and female labour into the deer industry. The result is that 75 per cent of the labour force is crowded into the beaver industry while only 25 per cent is employed in the deer industry. The wage for beaver hunters falls and the wage for deer hunters rises. The wage for white male labour rises relative to the wage for black labour and female labour because only white males are employed in the uncrowded deer industry which makes a positive 'profit' derived from the 'loss' incurred by black labour and female labour employed in the crowded beaver industry. The profit and loss are the short-run price effects of the institutionally induced change in the relative 'scarcity' of deer and beaver.

In the long run, since labour in the crowded beaver industry receives a lower wage, each individual purchases fewer goods as factors for the production of their hunting skills in subsequent production periods. The deer industry becomes relatively capital intensive and the beaver industry relatively time intensive. The aggregate output of deer rises and the aggregate output of beaver falls. The change in the composition of output is associated with an offsetting relative price change until a long-run equilibrium position is reached where higher wages are associated with higher productivities of individual time and lower wages with lower productivities.

It is interesting to contrast Smith's nation of homogeneous hunters with free entry and Walras' economy of heterogeneous savages with restricted entry:

I imagine a tribe of savages and a deer in a forest. The deer is a useful thing limited in quantity and hence subject to appropriation. This point once granted, nothing more needs to be said about it. To be sure, before the deer can be actually appropriated it has to be hunted or killed. Again, this side of the question need not detain us, nor need we stop to consider such correlated problems as arise in connection with the need to dress the deer and prepare it in the kitchen. Quite apart from all these aspects of man's relation to the deer, yet another question claims our attention; for whether the deer is still running about in the forest or has been killed, the question is: who shall have it? That is the point of view from which we are considering the problem of appropriation, for when it is looked at in this way, appropriation is seen to involve a relationship among persons. We need only carry our illustration one step further to make this clear. 'The deer belongs to the one who has killed it!' cries a young and active member of the tribe, adding, 'if you are too lazy or if your aim is not good enough, so much the worse for you!' An older, weaker member replies, 'No! The deer belongs to all of us to be shared equally. If there is only one deer in the forest, and you happen to be the first to catch sight of it, that is no reason why the rest of us should go without food' [1874, 77].

In Walras' tribe of savages, firstly, labour is restricted to the deer industry. Secondly, there is the assumption of only one deer in the forest. However, the deer belongs to a species which can be treated as a renewable resource. At any point in time the market price of the species in its natural environment is positive only under special conditions which imply a binding restriction on entry into the production of deer. Thirdly, if there is a complete set of Arrow-Debreu contingent markets to take account of uncertainty, luck in the time taken to catch the deer cannot determine who owns it. Finally, the contrast between an older, weaker member and a young and active member of the tribe suggests inequality due to age related productivity differences. We shall see in Chapter 3 that inequality by age requires binding restrictions on exchange between age groups. In a perfect capital market, which implies a complete set of forward markets, all individuals of an innately homogeneous society can be fully self supporting over the lifetime with access to equal lifetime incomes. Children borrow and the aged dissave by engaging in perfectly competitive intergenerational trade. The age related distributional dilemma implied by Walras does not arise in an environment with a complete set of perfectly competitive markets.

Thus, Walras – in his exposition of a theory of perfect competitions in which he argues that efficiency (his 'theory of industry') and distribution (his 'theory of property') are separable issues – pre-supposes apolitical restrictions of some kind and labour heterogeneity. When there are institutional restrictions on employment, wages can vary for innately homogeneous labour. Policies which remove institutional restrictions may increase efficiency and equality and so it cannot be said that efficiency and distribution are separable issues, nor that there is a trade-off between efficiency and equity, as in optimal tax theory. In the presence of binding institutional restrictions on employment, there are additional constraints on policy design which may reverse the conclusions of neoclassical theory.[20]

The example of crowding in Adam Smith's hunting economy illustrates the way in which, in modern economies, restrictions on entry into high income occupations can perpetuate inequality. In addition there may be restrictions on group formation within the crowded sector. The crowded sector cannot produce all goods which require local public goods as inputs as efficiently as the uncrowded sector if individuals within the crowded sector are not free to form groups of optimal size. If restrictions on entry into sub-groups within the crowded sector are binding, they influence the terms of trade between sectors. Constraints of this kind on household formation discussed in Chapter 4 offer an explanation for inequality between the market and household sectors.

The consideration of natural lifetime changes in labour productivity is also an important part of the analysis. While the tax incidence analysis indicates the conventional income tax-subsidy schemes can be ineffective, a crowding model with circular production suggests an alternative policy approach. The model offers a strong argument for measures directed towards improving the capital market by providing children with greater and more equal access to their potential lifetime incomes and, at the same time, for introducing measures which allocate a fairer share of legal resources to children to ensure that they are the beneficiaries of transfers made to them. It is suggested in Chapter 7 that removing capital market constraints in this way might be more effective than the tax-subsidy schemes usually advocated. If on reaching maturity children enter the market sector labour force with similar abilities, crowding inequality may become more readily observable and therefore increasingly difficult to maintain.

The analysis, in taking account of lifetime changes in labour productivity including changes prior to maturity, also recognises that every individual must borrow and save: that there is some level of capital accumulation associated with each age. From a life cycle approach it is clear that if there is inequality, the critical 'class' distinction is not between the owners of capital and of labour. Under institutional inequality the critical distinction is between groups of individuals, some of whom are subject to more binding constraints on mobility and consequently receive lower lifetime incomes and have less capital at each age, and others who are less restricted and consequently receive higher lifetime incomes and have more capital at each age. Whether or not those with more capital transfer a part of it from one generation to the next within a family group does not alter the model. The important issue is whether the mobility of endowments differs depending upon who owns the endowments.

The purpose of focusing on restrictions (i) to (iv) listed in section 1.2 is to allow us to encompass many aspects of the structure of inequality within an economy: inequality between market occupations caused by restrictions on entry into higher wage market activity; inequality between market and household labour due to restrictions on the size of households and on entry into the market sector, and the intergenerational perpetuation of inequality achieved by restrictions limiting a child's income opportunities to those of its parents. In choosing these particular restrictions it is not proposed that they adequately represent all institutional constraints operating in the economy. On the contrary, the purpose is to suggest that there is a diverse range of constraints and to show the extent to which the crowding mechanism described by the models can control prices, incomes and the incidence of taxation.

1.4 The specification of work and leisure and the effects of income taxation under institutional inequality

The effect of taxation when inequality is caused by institutional restrictions in one aspect of the analysis. A second important consideration is the specification of work and leisure. In Chapter 4 it is proposed that from a technical point of view, the appropriate definition of work is production for trade and the appropriate definition of leisure is production for own consumption. In any production period the individual has a fixed endowment of time that is allocated to production for trade and to production for own consumption. The term 'trade' is used to refer to any kind of social interaction or exchange between individuals. It is not limited to just the exchange of market goods or household services. All activity, irrespective of the group or sector within which it is performed, is partly work and partly leisure. This suggests we should question the interpretation of work as labour supply to market production and, as well, the distinction made between the firm as a producing agent and the household as a consuming agent.

The individual is recognised as the basic unit of analysis, and firms and households as groups of interacting or trading individuals. The division of activity into market and household sectors is identified as a purely institutional one. Production for consumption in the firm, such as job status and its attributes, is obvious. However, there is frequently some confusion about the nature of household production for trade. An individual produces for trade in the household sector when it is not the sole consumer of its product. An example is the rearing of children who, on maturity do not work for the individuals who produced them but instead for the market sector or for another household. A second example is the production of household services by a dependent spouse for the primary earner of a household. When institutional constraints limit females to employment in the household sector as dependent spouses of males employed in the market sector, there is job segregation on the basis of sex. The two segregated labour groups trade. Women produce household services which are purchased by men and subsequently they use their money wage incomes to purchase market goods. Thus there is monetised trading of household services.

When leisure in the household and in the firm is untaxable and wage incomes from trade within the market sector and within the household are untaxed, existing tax systems tax only monetised trade between the two sectors. Optimal tax theory takes into account the distortionary effects of the untaxability of leisure. However, no consideration seems to have been given to the incidence of income taxation as a tax on monetised trade between the market and household sectors when there is extensive market–household employment segregation by sex, and opportunities for leisure in the firm increase with the wage.

The analysis of tax incidence in Chapter 5 shows that the burden of income taxation as a trade tax can be shifted largely to labour in the household sector because of institutional constraints on the mobility of labour in the sector. The result depends on the premise that institutional restrictions on the entry of women into market sector jobs and on the size of households are binding: women are constrained to employment in the household sector and to employment in a particular production unit – the household – which cannot achieve the scale economies of firms. Consequently, unlike the market sector, the household sector cannot avoid a tax on trade between the two sectors by producing the same kinds of goods as the market sector for the same production costs. These conditions lead to the result that a greater part of the burden of income taxation can fall on the household sector, which is the low wage sector. The low wage group can pay absolutely more tax. This result has implications for the distribution of tax burdens among families. When higher wage groups in the market sector have greater opportunities for consumption in the firm, the burden of income taxation can be shifted to lower income families. Again, the incidence of taxation can be regressive. The results are contrasted with those obtained in the theory of optimal taxation.

The purpose of Chapter 6 is to stress that the effects of taxation depend upon the causes of inequality. When inequality is due to institutional constraints, the untaxability of leisure is not the only constraint on tax design. Even if leisure were taxable, the effective incidence of a progressive tax may be no less regressive. The rules for optimal taxation in a first best world are not appropriate when there are institutional constraints on job choices, irrespective of the feasibility of taxing production for own consumption. Tax incidence is shown to depend ultimately on how the decision to impose or increase taxes on higher income groups affects the power of those groups. If they have the power to maintain their wage positions, they might respond by imposing further restrictions on entry or by altering demand schedules. With this response to taxation the burden is shifted by increasing crowding, and this includes increasing underemployment and unemployment as traditionally defined. The theory implies that the structure of institutional inequality enables the burden of income taxation to be shifted by measures which reinforce inequality and the excess burden of institutional crowding. At best the kinds of tax-subsidy schemes widely advocated may be ineffective.

A further implication of institutional restrictions on the employment of women and on household production is examined in Chapter 7. With the rearing of children substantially limited to the household sector, it is argued that these restrictions encourage population growth. When the opportunity wage for women in the market sector is low, they may obtain higher wages by producing more children. In addition, when children and market goods are imperfect substitutes for men employed in the market sector, income taxation can reinforce the population growth effects of institutional restrictions on job opportunities for women. These population growth effects have implications for the longer term growth rate and for the structure of cyclical fluctuations in the growth rate of the economy.

2

Institutional inequality: a theory of crowding

2.1 Theories of trade and income distribution

Marginal productivity theory relates factor payments to marginal products. Inequality in wage incomes can arise if individual labour supplies or marginal value products differ. Marginal productivity theory however does not contain a theory of income distribution because there is no specification of the conditions under which supply and demand are determined. An additional assumption is required to introduce a theory of income distribution. The assumption chosen in neoclassical theory is that income differences are due to supply constraints imposed by innate or inherited endowments and tastes or by population size. The assumption underlying the crowding theory of inequality presented in this chapter is that institutional constraints on employment choices control factor demands and, in turn, marginal value products and endowments. The theory thus relies on marginal productivity theory but attributes inequality to institutional constraints.

The crowding model is a two sector model of trade which incorporates circular production functions. The model has certain features of the Ricardian trade model and of the Heckscher–Ohlin trade model. The fundamental difference is that the results are interpreted for institutional inequality. The Ricardian and Heckscher–Ohlin models can also be interpreted in the context of the same theory of income distribution to obtain conclusions which differ from those of neoclassical interpretations. The standard interpretation of the Ricardian model is a neoclassical theory of income distribution in an economy in which labour is the only factor of production. If labour is homogeneous and perfectly mobile between sectors in a closed economy, prices are proportional to labour times and there is equality in incomes. This result, the Ricardian 'labour theory of value', can be derived for a two sector economy with constant returns to scale and a fixed, fully employed labour force. Suppose that sector 1 produces x units of good X and sector 2 y units of good Y with fixed labour coefficients, a^x and a^y, respectively. Let p^x denote the price of good X, p^y the price of good Y, w^x the wage in sector 1 and w^y the wage in sector 2. Solving the competitive profit conditions yields the ratio of wages (the factoral terms of trade) as

$$\frac{w^x}{w^y} = \frac{p^x a^y}{p^y a^x}$$

Thus

$$w^x \gtrless w^y$$

as

$$\frac{p^x a^y}{p^y a^x} \gtrless 1$$

Marginal value products are equal if labour is homogeneous, and wage incomes are equal if, in addition, individual labour supplies to production for trade in each sector are the same.

According to neoclassical theory, marginal value products can differ if individuals possess different innate skills, inherited human capital or tastes. A wage differential between the sectors may be due to non-uniform differences in skills which impose a binding constraint and result in specialization (or job segregation) at the free trade equilibrium. Under this condition there is a unique wage rate in each sector. If non-uniform differences in skills impose a binding constraint but not specialization, wage differentials within a sector reflect skill levels. Alternatively, if individuals possess a taste for discrimination, this can impose the binding constraint necessary for a wage differential.[1]

Wage income inequality within or between sectors does not necessarily indicate a wage differential. In each sector individuals choose an allocation of time between production for trade and production for own consumption. If individuals in one sector have a relative preference for leisure, or if one job is more pleasant than another, a difference between wage incomes may be balanced by the value of production for own consumption, that is, by leisure. It is only 'full income' inequality which implies a wage differential.[2] In the trade literature the labour-leisure choice within a sector is not considered because work and leisure are assumed to be activities which can be separated. The full employment condition is restrictively interpreted to preclude leisure.

Ricardo assumed homogeneous labour within each country and so a wage differential could only occur between countries. The development of trade is attributed to non-uniform differences in skills which Ricardo termed differences in technologies between countries. However, if it is assumed that production exhibits constant returns to scale throughout, non-uniform heterogeneity in abilities or in tastes is needed to explain a division of labour and trade either between individuals in a closed economy or between countries.[3] The simple Ricardian trade model is criticised for its arbitrary assumption of different technologies, yet the same assumption is widely accepted as an explanation for wage differentials between jobs within a country. In the context of an institutional theory of inequality, the Ricardian model has a different interpretation. If binding institutional restrictions on job choices account for the development of trade, for employment segregation and for wage differentials, the gains from trade achieved by one sector are derived from losses incurred by the other, and the distortionary constraints impose an efficiency loss.

The Heckscher–Ohlin model is said to avoid the arbitrary assumption of non-uniform differences in labour coefficients of the Ricardian model. Capital (or land) is introduced as an additional factor of production. Labour can be homogeneous and technologies identical, and trade explained in terms of non-uniform differences in the factor endowments of the two countries. The model is a simplified version of a competitive general equilibrium model of a private ownership economy in which each country possesses initial endowments to which it has a legal right.[4] In applications of the model to the analysis of trade and income distribution within an economy, consumers rather than countries possess initial endowments. The Ricardian model, which also characterises the competitive equilibrium of a private ownership economy, has the distinguishing feature that each individual possesses endownments of skills. If labour is homogeneous, individuals have identical skills and there is equality because individual time is the constraint determining relative prices. In a two factor trade model which assumes that labour is homogeneous, income inequality can only be attributed to differences in capital endowments. Thus it can be argued that a multi-factor trade model is internally inconsistent if it assumes a homogeneous labour force and a complete set of perfectly competitive markets, and also permits a distribution of endowments at the beginning of a production period which can result in an unequal distribution of income.[5]

If there always exists a complete set of perfectly competitive markets and labour is homogeneous, an economy in which labour is initially the only factor of production cannot develop into a multi-factor economy characterized by an unequal distribution of income. If individuals have identical skills and tastes, they have the same relative preference for leisure and they save and invest at the same rate to acquire the same capital endowments at the beginning of every production period. With contingent markets to take account of uncertainty, luck cannot give rise to income differences, nor can scarce renewable or exhaustible resources. The existence of scarce resources with positive prices in natural environments requires binding restrictions on entry into the production of the resources. The introduction of scarce natural resources thus implies that factors are not perfectly mobile between sectors: that entry into sectors producing factors of production is constrained. Moreover, such constraints do not give rise to inequality if there always exists a complete set of contingent markets. For income inequality to develop within a homogeneous labour force, individuals must face differential restrictions on entry which alter the employment of factors. For example, the failure of the relevant contingent market may permit only those individuals who randomly discover a natural resource to legally own the rent from the resource. We have the same kind of condition as that which lies behind the notion of innate ability differences, viz., differential binding restrictions on entry into the production of ability. In examining the kinds of implicit assumptions underlying conventional interpretations of multi-factor trade analyses, Savage (1980) shows that models which treat capital as a scarce renewable resource are partial. In a general equilibrium context, the assumption of labour heterogeneity is required to explain inequality, as in the Ricardian model.

These problems underlying applications of a multi-factor trade model arise within the context of a neoclassical theory of distribution. The model has different implications when inequality in individual endownments is identified as the effect of institutional constraints on factor mobilities. The crowding theory of inequality presented below employs a trade model modified to represent the way in which inequality, once initiated, can be perpetuated and made to appear the result of given characteristics. The model suggests a mechanism whereby institutions control not only the distribution of income but, as well, individual endowments, factor intensities and elasticities of factor substitution.

2.2 Institutional restrictions and the organisation of production

When production exhibits constant returns in every period, two kinds of restrictions are required for institutional inequality. The first are restrictions on the kinds of goods which can be produced by sectors (or occupations or job positions within occupations). These restrictions determine sector demand schedules. The second are restrictions on the quantities of factors employed in sectors.[6] For example, in a professional or licenced occupation, the demand schedule for the services of the occupation might be controlled by legal restrictions on the production of close substitutes by individuals outside the occupation. Numbers might be limited by annual quotas on the intake of students into training institutions. There are in general two ways in which the wage for an occupation can be changed. Demand schedules may be altered by tighter legal restrictions on the production of close substitutions by 'non-professionals'[7] or, alternatively, entry may be limited.

For the purpose of the present analysis, it is assumed that, through the political evolution of our institutions (particularly of the legal system) and of social custom, the economy has been divided into professional occupations and managerial job categories, and into household and market activities. Each sector has a negatively sloped demand schedule which cannot be altered during the period of analysis. Only employment can be varied. Factors employed in each sector can be altered by adjusting restrictions on entry. Clearly, there are other restrictions which operate in practice when high-wage groups are observed to exercise controls on the demand for their services. Nevertheless, there are many instances where the assumption of fixed demand schedules is fairly realistic. It may take time to introduce laws which define and restrict the production of certain goods and services by individuals who do not have specified professional and trade qualifications. In contrast, numbers may be changed fairly readily when occupation groups have the legal power to alter quotas by agreement within the group and to effect the change by limiting the number of new entrants into training institutions or by lengthening the training period, rather than by eliminating current members.

The model of crowding is formulated using a competitive Walrasian framework but, in contrast to the usual interpretation of price taking, it is not assumed agents always behave as price takers. Employment in each sector depends on the distribution of power and may alter in response to a change in policy for political reasons. An alternative approach would be a non-Walrasian model in which sector employment is an endogenous variable. For example, an occupation group might be represented as a revenue maximising cartel[8] on the premise that all members of the group achieve a higher wage by explicit collusion. A cartel model of this kind and the 'competitive' model of institutional inequality proposed here both depend on the premise that there are politically more powerful groups who can restrict entry into their occupations. Both models rest on an a priori assumption that there is an unequal distribution of power which, per se, has no effect on productivities but is used to distort productivities. Neither model represents the way in which the power structure has developed; it is simply taken as given, although there may be references to the historical origins of the power structure in the discussion of applications of either model.

2.3   Production functions and equilibrium conditions

The model of crowding is presented for a simple two-sector economy. However, the implications for a multi-sector economy are easily interpreted. In the first period there is free entry. The identically skilled or equipped individuals are perfectly mobile between sectors. This implies there are no short run scarcities of resources; that technology, the identical tastes and the time of each individual impose the only binding constraints. Wage income is invested in capital goods which are not sector specific: investment is in capital which is homogeneous. Thus the terms 'capital', 'human capital' and 'skilled labour' can be used interchangeably.

We assume each individual works in only one of the two sectors. Sector 1 produces good X and sector 2 produces good Y. The production of good X and good Y requires capital, k, and time, l. Constant returns to scale production functions for each individual in sector 1 producing good X and in sector 2 producing good Y take the form[9]

$$x = X(k^1, l^1) \quad x_k, x_l > 0; \quad x_{kk}, x_{ll} > 0$$

$$y = Y(k^2, l^2) \quad y_k, y_l > 0; \quad y_{kk}, y_{ll} > 0$$

where

x is the output of good X by an individual in sector 1.
k^1 is the capital of an individual employed in sector 1.
l^1 is the time the individual works in sector 1.
y is the output of good Y by an individual in sector 2.
k^2 is the capital of an individual employed in sector 2.
l^2 is the time the individual works in sector 2.

Since each individual can work in only one sector, the time of each individual allocated to production activity is fixed in each production period. Thus

$$\bar{l}^1 = \bar{l}^2$$

and the above production functions can be re-written as

$$x = x(k^1) \quad x_k > 0; \ x_{kk} < 0 \qquad (2.1)$$

$$y = y(k^2) \quad y_k > 0; \ y_{kk} < 0 \qquad (2.2)$$

The wage, which includes payment to capital and time, is used to purchase good X and good Y. With circular production functions, the two goods are factors for the production of capital. Constant returns to scale production functions for an individual's capital in each sector are given by

$$k^1 = k^1(x^1, y^1) \qquad k_x^1, k_y^1 > 0; \quad k_{xx}^1, k_{yy}^1 < 0 \tag{2.3}$$

$$k^2 = k^2(x^2, y^2) \qquad k_x^2, k_y^2 > 0; \quad k_{xx}^2, k_{yy}^2 < 0 \tag{2.4}$$

respectively, where

> x^1, y^1 are the demands for good X and good Y, respectively, by an individual employed in sector 1.
>
> x^2, y^2 are the demands for good X and good Y, respectively, by an individual employed in sector 2.

Utility is derived from social status and its attributes. Social status depends on capital and so utility is a function of capital:

$$u^1 = u^1(k^1)$$

$$u^2 = u^2(k^2)$$

If we choose y as numeraire we can let p denote the price ratio and w the wage ratio. Units can be chosen such that in the first period when there are no restrictions on mobility

$$p = w = 1$$

which implies an equal society.

Let group 1 represent the individuals employed in sector 1 and group 2 the individuals employed in sector 2. If n denotes the number of individuals in group 1 and m the number in group 2, the sector employment ratio, γ, is defined as

$$\gamma = \frac{m}{n} \quad m, n > 0$$

Demand functions are given by

$$x^1 = x^1(p, px) \qquad x_p^1 < 0, x_{px}^1 > 0$$

$$x^2 = x^2(p, y) \qquad x_p^2 < 0, x_y^2 > 0$$

$$y^1 = y^1(p, px) \qquad y_p^1, y_{px}^1 > 0$$

$$y^2 = y^2(p, y) \qquad y_p^2, y_y^2 > 0$$

The equilibrium conditions for supply and demand can be written as

$$x^1(p, px) + \gamma x^2(p, y) = x \tag{2.5}$$

$$y^1(p, px) + \gamma y^2(p, y) = \gamma y \tag{2.6}$$

Budget constraints take the form

$$px^1(p, px) + y^1(p, px) = px \tag{2.7}$$

$$px^2(p, y) + y^2(p, y) = y \tag{2.8}$$

From (2.5) to (2.8) we obtain the trade relationship

$$p\gamma x^2(p, y) - y^1(p, px) = 0 \tag{2.9}$$

2.4 Institutional restrictions on employment

We now introduce restrictions on mobility between the two sectors. The restrictions determine the number of individuals employed in each sector and hence the total input of time to each sector. In subsequent periods, the restrictions apply both to the mobility of individuals and their capital. In other words, individuals must invest their accumulated incomes in the sector in which they are employed. The practical implication of this assumption is that in a multi-sector economy institutional restrictions on individuals usually apply with respect to an individual's job and investment opportunities.

Let all individuals be distinguishable on the basis of a number of observable characteristics which, per se, have no effect on productivities but allow the sector employment ratio to vary depending on which characteristics are chosen for the classification. Once subdivided into two groups the following institutional restrictions are imposed

 (i) individuals in group 1 must work in sector 1 only; and,
(ii) individuals in group 2 must work in sector 2 only.

The price and wage effects of a change in the sector employment ratio, γ, are derived for two time periods:

(a) the short run: a period of time during which output per individual in sectors 1 and 2 is fixed at $\bar{x}$ and $\bar{y}$, respectively; and

(b) the long run: a period of time during which output per individual adjusts to the short run relative price
change via investment.

The relevant production functions for the short run are (2.1) and (2.2)
where each individual's human capital is fixed at $\bar{k}^1$ or $\bar{k}^2$ so that each
individual's output is fixed at $\bar{x}$ or $\bar{y}$. In the long run, k^1 and k^2 are
variable. Human capital is a function of the individual's purchases of
good X and good Y, as indicated by equations (2.3) and (2.4), and the
quantities purchased depend on the price and wage in each sector and
so depend on the short run relative price change caused by the
restrictions.

2.5   Crowding in the short run

The short run effects of an institutional change in the sector employment ratio can be illustrated for a closed economy where, prior to any
restrictions, each sector employs the same number of equally skilled
individuals. Suppose the individuals are distinguishable by non-
economic characteristics of sex and colour. Half the population is
white and half is black and in each of these groups there is the same
number of males and females. Let group 1 represent white males and
group 2 black males and all females. The restrictions allow only white
males, who comprise 25 per cent of the labour force, to work in sector
1. Figure 2.1 describes the locus of equilibria with changes in the
sector employment ratio, γ, for the special case where each sector
always employs the two goods in the proportions in which they are
produced.

Once the restrictions are imposed, the output of sector 1 falls by 50
per cent as indicated by $n\bar{x} - n'\bar{x}$ because the restrictions require that
the number of individuals employed in sector 1 fall by 50 per cent. In
contrast, the output of sector 2 rises by 50 per cent as indicated by
$m'\bar{y} - m\bar{y}$ because the fall in employment in sector 1 is absorbed by
sector 2. Since capital is fixed at $\bar{k}^1$ and $\bar{k}^2$ in the short run, output per
unit of time is fixed at $\bar{x}$ in sector 1 and at $\bar{y}$ in sector 2. With fixed
labour coefficients the ratio of sector outputs is equal to the ratio of
sector employments. Sector 2 now produces three times as much as
sector 1. At the new output levels the price of X rises to p'.

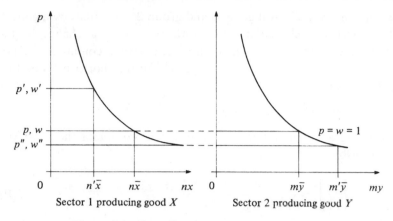

Figure 2.1   Crowding in a two sector economy

Each individual in sector 1 makes a profit of $(p' - p)\bar{x}$ which is acquired as a wage increase from w to w'. Each individual in sector 2 makes a loss of $(p - p'')\bar{y}$ which is incurred as a wage fall from w to w''.[10] Since each sector employs the two goods in the proportion in which they are produced, the price ratio, p, increases to three. Thus, prior to restrictions, labour coefficients are the same in both sectors and one unit of X exchanges for one unit of Y. After the restrictions labour coefficients are still the same but one unit of X exchanges for three units of Y. With this change in marginal value products, the wage in sector 1 is three times the wage in sector 2. We observe job specialization and unequal wages because of institutional restrictions. Notice that if both sectors always purchase the goods in the same proportions, on a cross sectional basis preferences would appear homothetic. In addition, because of the assumptions employed, the price change does not alter individual labour supply to production for trade in each sector.

This example illustrates crowding in terms of the effects of a change in aggregate supplies of the two goods. Alternatively, the change in price with respect to a change in the employment ratio can be seen to result from a shift in the demand for the output of each individual. As γ rises the demand for the output of a group 1 individual shifts out and the demand for the output of a group 2 individual shifts back.[11] As the price of X rises there are the usual substitution and income effects and, as well, there is an income distribution effect because group 1 individuals own good X and group 2 individuals own good Y. The short run change in price with respect to a change in the employment ratio can be derived from equilibrium conditions (2.5) or (2.6), or from the trade relation in (2.9).[12] In the short run, condition (2.6) becomes

$$y^1(p, p\bar{x}) + \gamma y^2(p, \bar{y}) - \gamma\bar{y} = 0$$

Assuming a unique interior solution for p, we obtain the short run relationship

$$\left[\frac{\partial p}{\partial \gamma}\right]_S = \frac{y^1}{\gamma(y_p^1 + \bar{x}y_{p\bar{x}}^1 + \gamma y_p^2)} > 0 \tag{2.10}$$

as $y_{p\bar{x}}^1 > 0$; that is, the change in the price ratio with respect to a change in the employment ratio is positive provided the foreign good is a normal good. This is the standard result for a simple international trade model.

Alternatively, condition (2.5) which, in the short run, becomes

$$x^1(p, p\bar{x}) + \gamma x^2(p, \bar{y}) - \bar{x} = 0$$

yields the short run relationship

$$\left[\frac{\partial p}{\partial \gamma}\right]_S = \frac{-x^2}{x_p^1 + \bar{x}x_{p\bar{x}}^1 + \gamma x_p^2} > 0 \tag{2.11}$$

as $y_{p\bar{x}}^1 > 0$.[13] Terms x_p^1 and x_p^2 are the gross substitution effects of a change in the price ratio on individual demands. The income distribution effect on demand is represented by $\bar{x}x_{p\bar{x}}^1$. The denominator thus contains the two effects opposite in direction, on the income of an individual in sector 1 (the home country) in response to a change in the price ratio (the terms of trade).

Observe that the sum, $x_p^1 + \bar{x}x_{p\bar{x}}^1$, is the change in a group 1 individual's demand for its own product. It is thus the change in production for own consumption or leisure by an individual in group 1 in response to a change in the wage rate. From this point of view, x_p^1 can be interpreted as the work–leisure substitution effect and $\bar{x}x_{p\bar{x}}$ as the income effect of a change in the wage rate. The special case where $x_p^1 + \bar{x}x_{p\bar{x}}^1 = 0$ implies that each individual retains a fixed proportion of production for own consumption. Under this condition individual labour supply to production for trade in each sector is fixed.

In (2.10) and (2.11) we have the general short run result that the price ratio p, and hence the wage ratio, w, increase (decrease) as γ increases (decreases); that is

$$w = p \gtrless 1$$

as

$$\partial \gamma \gtrless 0$$

There is employment segregation and a wage differential because of a binding institutional constraint on employment. If the change in the sector employment ratio is positive, sector 2 becomes crowded, and if it is negative sector 1 becomes crowded. If there is no change in the sector employment ratio, there is segregation but not inequality because neither restriction is binding.

2.6   Crowding in the long run

In the long run individual productivities depend on wages in previous periods. In response to a short run change in the relative wage, the individual whose wage declines is relatively less productive tomorrow than the individual whose wage increases. With a binding restriction on mobility between sectors, changes in labour productivities alter aggregate levels of output from each sector. If, as indicated in Figure 2.1, restrictions crowd sector 2 so that it produces three times as much output as sector 1, and one unit of X exchanges for three units of Y, the wage in sector 1 is three times the wage in sector 2. Sector 1 contains only 25 per cent of the population but earns 50 per cent of aggregate income. With constant returns to scale in (2.3) and (2.4), a sector 1 individual acquires three times the human capital of a sector 2 individual.

In response to investment in human capital, the output of sector 1 increases over time. If time and capital were perfect substitutes there would be constant marginal productivity of capital (x_{kk}, $y_{kk} = 0$ in (2.1) and (2.2)) and the sector output ratio would return to the precrowding ratio, although the wage in sector 1 would be three times the wage in sector 2 because a sector 1 individual becomes three times as productive. However, in any production period each individual's time is fixed. There are diminishing returns to capital (x_{kk}, $y_{kk} < 0$) and so as k^1/l^1 increases relative to k^2/l^2 there is an increasing excess burden. The long run sector output ratio does not equal the precrowding ratio. This imposes an excess burden in the production of capital (k_{xx}, $k_{yy} < 0$ in (2.3) and (2.4)). Long run wages reflect crowding induced differences in individual productivities and the wage differential between sectors can be large even when the relative price change is small. Thus, if institutional restrictions on mobility are considered unimportant, the economy can appear to be efficient and the wage differential to be determined by the given characteristics of individuals in a competitive labour market.

The long run change in price with respect to γ can be derived from equilibrium condition (2.6). Assuming a unique interior solution for p, we obtain the long run relationship

$$\left[\frac{\partial p}{\partial \gamma}\right]_L = \frac{y^1}{\gamma \left(y_p^1 + y_{px}^1 \dfrac{\partial px}{\partial p} + \gamma y_p^2 + \gamma \dfrac{\partial y}{\partial p}(y_y^2 - 1) \right)} > 0 \qquad (2.12)$$

for $y_y^2 < 1$, y_{px}^1, $\dfrac{\partial x}{\partial p} > 0$, $\dfrac{\partial y}{\partial p} < 0$.[14] The long run change in price in response to a change in the employment ratio is positive provided the foreign good is a normal good and, in addition, there are diminishing marginal products.

Alternatively, from equilibrium condition (2.5) we obtain[15]

$$\left[\frac{\partial p}{\partial \gamma}\right]_L = \frac{-x^2}{x_p^1 + x_{px}^1 \dfrac{\partial px}{\partial p} - \dfrac{\partial x}{\partial p} + \gamma \left(x_p^2 + x_y^2 \dfrac{\partial y}{\partial p} \right)} > 0$$

As in the short run relationship in (2.11), the terms x_p^1 and x_p^2 are gross substitution effects. Whereas in the short run a change in the distribution of income affects only demands, in the long run there are changes in output. For an individual in group 1, the demand and output effects of a change in the distribution of income are captured by $\left(x_{px}^1 \dfrac{\partial px}{\partial p} - \dfrac{\partial x}{\partial p} \right)$ and for an individual in group 2 by $\left(x_y^2 \dfrac{\partial y}{\partial p} \right)$. The denominator can also be interpreted in terms of labour-leisure choices.

Since the long run change in price is less than the short run change, we have the general long run result that

$$w \gtreqless p \gtreqless 1$$

as

$$\partial \gamma \gtreqless 0$$

The wage in the crowding sector increases more than the price of the good because each individual employed in the sector becomes more productive.

The model shows how binding institutional restrictions can, in the long run, induce differences in factor intensities between sectors. Crowding sectors become more capital intensive and crowded sectors time intensive. High wage individuals accumulate more capital. They are more productive. Thus we see how factor endowment ratios and factor intensities can be controlled by institutions, and inequality perpetuated indefinitely in an environment which appears to be perfectly competitive or to allow 'free trade'.

We can consider some implications of relaxing the investment assumption and allowing a hierarchy of investment opportunities. Suppose there are three sectors distinguished by the extent of crowding: a high wage sector, a middle wage sector and a low wage sector. If it is relatively easy to restrict investment in human capital but not in physical capital, we might expect the highest wage jobs to be those using human capital, where 'human capital' refers not only to education in the conventional sense but also to access and control of information. In the middle and low wage sectors we might expect to see physical capital investment. Under these conditions it is more difficult to restrict the entry of capital into low wage sectors. If the high wage group invests in the middle wage sector and the wage in the sector is set by a labour union which is not fully effective in simultaneously restricting the entry of 'foreign' capital, as investment in the sector rises, price falls. Employment in the sector must fall to maintain a rigid wage, and the only alternative employment is in the low wage sector where incomes are reduced in response to an increase in employment.

Thus, the highest wage group, owning a proportionally greater share of capital, may initiate and control 'unemployment' and differences in capital-time ratios. The formulation of the model can be extended to explain rising unemployment with technological change in terms of political controls imposed by the most powerful individuals in the society who, through the use of the institutions, can appear to behave as price takers. In contrast, conventional theory, by ignoring institutions controlling income differences, can attribute differences in factor intensities to non-institutional requirements of production, and differences in individual incomes to given endowments.

3

The life cycle and institutional inequality

3.1 Life cycle changes in productivity and inequality

The preceding analysis treats all individuals as innately identical adults whose productivities differ because of institutional crowding. This chapter introduces changes in individual productivities over the life cycle. The innate productivity of an individual increases during childhood and may decline in old age, and the existence of each individual depends upon reproduction decisions made by the previous generation. The aim of this chapter is to identify the effects of crowding among adults in a society where, for institutional reasons, children are to a large extent 'dependent' upon parents. Again, individuals are assumed to be innately identical in productivities and tastes, but on a lifetime basis: in the absence of binding institutional restrictions, individuals of the same age are homogeneous in abilities and tastes. The discussion abstracts from problems of uncertainty.[1]

A fundamental feature of a life cycle approach is that the individual is recognised as the basic unit of analysis. In optimal tax models which specify leisure as untaxable, the individual is also the unit of analysis, irrespective of the formation of households or other social groups.[2] In a single period model where the only source of income is wage income, inequality is attributed to the present characteristics of individuals. In a multi-period model where capital is introduced as savings from wage income of present and past generations, the theory is extended to take account of certain aspects of the life cycle and of intergenerational transfers. The emphasis is usually on saving for retirement. But a fundamental feature of the life cycle is that productivity is relatively low prior to maturity. Consequently, during

33

childhood the individual borrows from its future income. The implications of this for policy design in an imperfect capital market are frequently neglected.

Applications of the two-factor trade model to the analysis of tax incidence do not focus on the individual. To derive a correspondence between the factor distribution of tax burdens and the individual distribution, individuals must be grouped according to their factor endowments. To the extent an individual earns wage income, the individual is classified as labour, and to the extent that the individual earns capital, the individual is classified as a capitalist. If labour is assumed to be homogeneous, inequality depends on capital ownership, and the theory of inequality underlying the two factor trade model is a theory of capital accumulation. The life cycle model of savings and the class savings model are considered polar hypotheses. The latter attributes capital accumulation to savings from profit earned from capital. The initial distribution of capital is given and profit may include a pure rent component. In these respects the theory is analogous to a given characteristics theory of inequality. The Kaldor savings function is an intermediate thesis which attributes capital accumulation partly to savings from capital and partly to savings from wage income.

When individual productivity changes with age, a life cycle approach is appropriate. A model based solely on a given endowments theory of inequality ignores not only institutional inequality but differences in endowments and incomes associated with age. Section 3.2 discusses the implications of changes in individual productivity over the life cycle when there are no binding institutional constraints and the production of goods exhibits constant returns to scale.[3] Under these conditions individuals from different stages of the life cycle trade time-dated goods. There is intergenerational trade because individuals currently in the 'prime age' stage of the life cycle have a comparative advantage in producing present goods. Children have a comparative advantage in producing future goods. From this perspective each individual can be seen to be fully self supporting over the lifetime. Children are neither investment goods nor consumption items of parents but equal trading partners on a lifetime basis, provided there are no institutional constraints distorting intergenerational trade within or outside the family.

In modern economies intergenerational trade has to some extent been taken outside the family by State provision of education and by cash transfers to the aged. Nevertheless, children remain largely dependent upon parents. Their access to future lifetime income is thus constrained to access through the family. This institutional arrangement can be non-distortionary, but in section 3.3 it is proposed that when there is crowding inequality among parents, a family system of access to income for children imposes a binding constraint on the children of parents in crowded occupations. The second round effects of crowding enable inequality among parents to be reproduced among children. Section 3.4 introduces scale economies and the formation of families as a response to local public goods such as 'caring'. It is proposed that institutional constraints on family and household formation contribute to crowding inequality and to the distortion of intergenerational trade.

3.2   Intergenerational trade

In a simple life cycle model the individual maximises lifetime utility subject to the constraint imposed by lifetime income. Lifetime utility is represented as a function of consumption levels at each stage of the life cycle. The solution to the individual's problem gives the lifetime consumption profile and simultaneously determines the rate of growth. Savings are invested in human and physical capital and determine the biological growth rate and the per capita growth rate of human and physical capital. In a model in which labour is the only factor of production, income at any stage of the life cycle depends on labour productivity at that stage. If labour is homogeneous and there exists a complete set of markets, individuals of the same age receive equal current incomes and equal lifetime incomes. The standard analysis treats the individual in the prime age of the life cycle as the decision maker.

In the analysis of fertility two approaches can be distinguished. Models of steady-state population growth can be seen as a formal development of the old age security hypothesis. Prime age adults make savings and investment decisions to maximise utility during the remainder of life which has two states: the present working stage and retirement. The Samuelson (1958) model, which assumes constant returns to scale and no capital,[4] shows that the income available for the retired, whether from optimal social security or private intergenerational loans, increases as population growth increases. The higher the rate of population growth, the higher the per capita steady-state consumption. However, Samuelson not only omits physical capital but also omits loans to children, stating that 'children are a part of their parents' consumption, and we take no note of them' (p. 468). Whether population growth allows more or less steady-state consumption depends on the ratio of consumption by the aged to consumption by children. Diamond (1965) and Samuelson (1968) introduce capital, which is analogous to introducing investment in children. While population growth can have the advantage of giving the retired more working individuals to support them, it can have the disadvantage of reducing consumption goods per capita because of the need to 'widen' capital in proportion to population growth. Samuelson (1975a) examines the trade-off between additional income for the retired and the need to 'widen' capital with population growth, and concludes that there may exist an optimum intermediate rate of population growth.[5] The analysis by Deardorff (1976) identifies conditions under which an intermediate rate of population growth minimises per capita welfare. Samuelson (1976) suggests, however, that the conditions are unlikely to hold: that an intermediate rate of population growth is more likely to be an optimum.

The second approach is based on the observation that parents enjoy having children. This is taken as evidence that fertility is not solely dependent upon a return from investment in children. In addition, parents and children have interdependent utilities. Parents' utility is a function of the goods they consume and of their childrens' consumption (Neher (1971)), and of their childrens' childrens' consumption (Razin and Ben-Zion (1975)). Some studies suggest a household utility function. In an effort to explain the influence of family income on fertility, the models in Becker (1960), Mincer (1962), De Tray (1973) and Becker and Lewis (1973) employ a family welfare function with three arguments: the quantity of children, the quality of children and other goods. All are assumed to be normal goods. The observation that higher income families tend to have fewer children is explained in terms of the relative size of the 'true' income effect and the substitution effect. Since, as income goes up, the demand for child quality increases, the price of children increases. The observed change in the number of children with a rise in parent income therefore depends on the relationship between the size of the 'true' income effect and the size of the substitution effect due to the increase in the relative price of children. Becker argues that his theory generalises that of Malthus (and of the classical economists who predicted a rate of population growth which would keep the real wage at subsistence) by relating the quantity of children to the quality of children to explain small or negative changes in family size with increasing family income.[6]

The two approaches are easily integrated. Moreover, both are open to the criticism that in focusing on decision making by prime age adults they reflect institutional phenomena and fail to adequately take account of children as utility maximizing individuals at an early stage of the life cycle. To examine these issues we can consider an economy with production functions of the form represented by (2.1) to (2.4). We have an economy with capital. Individuals are innately identical and, in the absence of institutional restrictions, they receive equal lifetime incomes. Individual time is the only binding constraint (there are no diminishing returns to resources such as land) and so the production of goods exhibits constant returns to scale and individual time can be treated as the only factor of production in the long run. Under these conditions, lifetime consumption is constrained by the present value of lifetime output as in the conventional one factor model. Lifetime output is, in effect, the only scarce exhaustible resource available for consumption.

Suppose that each innately identical individual lives 80 years with a lifetime pattern of productivity which can be subdivided into three life cycle stages: Stage A: ages 0 to 20; stage B: ages 20+ to 60; and stage C: ages 60+ to 80. In stage A the individual consumes more than it produces, in stage B the individual produces more than it consumes and in stage C the individual again consumes more than it produces. Figure 3.1 illustrates the three stages for a representative individual. The lifetime production profile indicates that individual productivity increases during childhood, reaches a maximum in stage B and declines in the second half of stage B and in stage C. The consumption path is represented by a horizontal line on the assumption that consumption levels at any time are equal for all age groups: Children and adults may consume different goods because of age differences in tastes, but each individual, irrespective of age, has the same level of consumption. When Figure 3.1 depicts the production and consumption profiles of a representative individual in sector 1 producing good X, the individual's full income at each age is equal to output weighted by prices at time t, $p(t)x(t)$. Lifetime full income is represented by the area under the production profile. Full expenditure at each age is given by leisure goods and traded goods weighted by prices at time t, $p(t)x^1(t) + y^1(t)$, where x^1 and y^1 are realised demands. The present value of full lifetime consumption cannot exceed the present value of full lifetime income, and the diagram illustrates the special case where the areas under the production and consumption profiles are equal, indicating a zero interest rate.

If we choose individuals of ages coinciding with stage B as the decision makers, this is an institutional matter. For the representative individual the problem is to maximize lifetime utility which depends on consumption in all stages of the life cycle. If the optimum consumption profile is horizontal and productivity varies with age as indicated in Figure 3.1, the solution to the individual's problem is achieved by transferring output or purchasing power from stage B to stages A and C. During childhood the individual must borrow from its future income and during stage B the individual repays debts incurred in childhood and saves for stage C. This intergeneration borrowing and lending can be viewed as intergenerational trade. The individual in stage A trades future goods it will produce in stage B for present goods. The stage B individual, in addition to meeting commit-

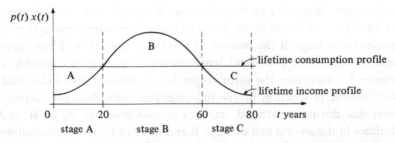

Figure 3.1 Individual lifetime production and consumption profiles

ments made in stage A, trades present goods for future goods for consumption in stage C. If there exists a complete set of forward markets (that is, markets upon which present goods can be sold for future goods and future goods sold for present goods) the intertemporal competitive equilibrium is Pareto efficient. By competitive intergenerational trade the individual is fully self-supporting over the lifetime even though such independence is not possible at all stages of the life cycle. With innately identical individuals there is income equality within every generation because the perfect capital market allows every child to borrow from the older generation at the same rate of interest. Under these conditions, irrespective of whether intergenerational trade is limited to trade between parents and children within the family, all individuals become equally productive adults who repay the same debts incurred in childhood and save the same amounts for old age.

Under the assumption of constant returns to scale this intergenerational trade is analogous, from a technical view point, to trade between countries as represented by a conventional international trade model. Two age groups engage in intergenerational trade because life cycle related skills give each a comparative advantage in the production of goods produced at different times. Only goods can be traded in an economy which does not permit slavery. Reproduction decisions in this context involve a decision to generate a trading partner. To take account of parents' enjoyment of their children we can extend the analysis for all kinds of goods. Children and parents differ not only with respect to comparative advantages in producing goods at a particular date, but in comparative advantages in producing different kinds of goods. In particular, children possess a comparative advantage in producing goods which give 'psychic' satisfaction to parents. Whether some children possess a comparative advantage in producing necessities and others in producing luxuries depends on the relationship between child quality and parent income. In an economy in which intergenerational trade is limited to trade between parents and children within the family, child quantity and quality decisions reflect parent choices concerning trading partners.

Focusing on relations between parents and children as trade relations serves to emphasise that the child, as well as the parent, is an individual decision maker in its own right. Lifetime consumption and savings profiles, and the growth of population and capital, can only be optimal if institutions do not distort trade relations between parents and children. To guarantee this it is necessary to protect the trading position of children. Yet observation suggests that in modern economies legal resources are employed primarily for the purpose of protecting the trading interests of prime age adults employed in the market sector who, for institutional reasons, are the more powerful decision makers in the economy.

The same principle of intergenerational trade holds irrespective of the equilibrium rate of growth or rate of interest. A positive (or negative) equilibrium rate of interest arising from biological growth can be interpreted as a price effect of intergenerational crowding. The higher the rate of population growth, the more stage A labour is crowded by stage B labour (or conversely). Depending upon the ratio of stage A to stage C per capita consumption, with population growth there are relatively more (or less) producers of future goods than of present goods. Consequently the price of present goods rises (falls) as population growth increases.

A life cycle trade approach identifies, in principle, age related differences in capital endowments. At the beginning of any production period individuals possess unequal capital endowments but this does not necessarily reflect inequality. In an environment which allows an efficient intertemporal competitive equilibrium, the introduction of a tax on income from capital can be seen as a distortionary tax on intergenerational trade. It discourages the individual from transferring income from stage B of the life cycle to stages A and C. In this context, a two-factor general equilibrium analysis of the incidence of a tax on capital has implications for the distribution of the burden among age groups. Harberger (1962) proposes that the effects of capital taxation on savings be examined, implying that if the tax reduced the return on capital it would reduce savings and investment. A tax on all income from capital would, however, tax savings for retirement and borrowing for investment in human capital for children. The tax can be expected to reduce capital formation for children and the retired but to increase it for adults in stage B, given circular production functions. While the tax is likely to distort investment in capital between age groups, the effect on aggregate savings and investment and on the rate of interest would depend on age group elasticities of demand for borrowing.[7] Although a tax on income from capital can be distortionary, it may be appropriate if crowding sectors can acquire renewable resources earning pure rents. Later chapters examine the effects of income taxation under institutional inequality and the results suggest that income taxation, unaccompanied by policy measures to alter the power structure, is unlikely to be effective in redistributing endowments or incomes.

3.3   Intergenerational trade and institutional inequality

When intergenerational trade is constrained to trade between parents and children of the same family, the system can be non-distortionary as already noted. However, when there is crowding inequality among adults, a family system of access to income for children becomes a mechanism for perpetuating inequality from one generation to the next because of second round effects on the productivities of children. If institutional restrictions cause crowding inequality only among adults, and innately homogeneous children face a perfect capital market, they emerge from stage A equally productive. To sustain crowding inequality in stage B and later in stage C, discrimination is required in the employment of equally productive new entrants to stage B. Children of high income parents would become the next generation of high income earners only if the discrimination were always in their favour. Were entry into high wage jobs random and children chose to insure against the event of employment in a crowded job, the inequality in stages B and C would disappear. There would be an excess burden associated with crowding but no inequality.

In the presence of institutional inequality among adults, a family system of access to income for children distorts the capital market so that parents in crowding sectors can invest more in their children than parents in crowded sectors. Consequently, children do not enter stage B equally productive, nor randomly enter crowding or crowded occupations. In studies of taxation a family system of access to income is generally supported on the basis of the premise that inequality between parents and therefore between children from different families is apolitical or, if it is institutional, this does not alter the analysis. In addition, it is widely accepted that children are solely consumption items of parents and should therefore be supported by parents.[8] Although human capital theory recognises that parent income affects the achievements of children,[9] in attributing inequality to the contribution parents make to the human capital or wealth of their children, the theory gives no further indication of underlying causes of inequality than explanations in terms of innate abilities or luck. The same comment can be made in respect of theories which attribute differences in lifetime earnings profiles to imperfect information about abilities. Individuals are assumed to possess different but unknown innate abilities and, as a result, not to know their optimum rates of investment in human capital. Such imperfect information theories are based indirectly on a given characteristics theory of inequality.

Once children of parents in crowding sectors become more productive, the education system screens[10] for induced ability differences and labels each child accordingly. When the labels determine entry into high wage occupations, we have the familiar phenomenon of children inheriting their parents' occupation class as well as their wealth.[11] The lifetime income effects of a family system of access to income for children with crowding in adult occupations is illustrated in Figure 3.2 for an economy with two occupation classes, the rich in sector 1 and the poor in sector 2. Productivity is increased for the child of rich parents and lowered for the child of poor parents. The difference in child quality by income can be defined as the difference between productivities in stage A. With crowding inequality in stage B, the productivity patterns continue over the lifetime as indicated,

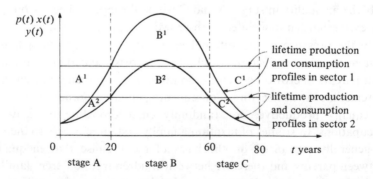

Figure 3.2   Lifetime production and consumption profiles in a two-sector economy with crowding inequality

and they produce corresponding differences in consumption levels for rich and poor. A family system of access to income for children with institutional crowding among parents can thus be seen to enable children of rich parents to 'inherit' greater productivity than the children of poor parents. Since it induces distortions in the production of goods and sustains inequality, a policy to equalise incomes for children could, if effective, increase efficiency and reduce inequality simultaneously.

3.4 Family formation: a response to local public goods or to institutional constraints?

Under constant returns to scale the neoclassical explanation for trade is non-uniform differences in endowments. This implies that intergenerational trade within the family is a purely institutional phenomenon. If it is argued that there are additional considerations in the case of family formation, such as interdependencies associated with 'caring', family formation may be seen as a response to economies of scale. An explanation of group formation in terms of economies of scale is provided by the theory of local public goods.[12] In a perfectly competitive environment, individuals form groups such as the family, the firm, the local community or club, in response to scale economies; that is, to gain access to local public goods. They may form different kinds of groups to produce different local public goods, and for the family 'caring' may be an important example. The existence of a local public good implies that, up to an optimum group size, there are gains from interaction or trade within a group. At the optimum group size, economies of scale are exhausted. This provides a theory of group formation irrespective of whether the group is the family and trade occurs between family members, or the group is an international community and trade takes place between countries. In contrast to the international trade model, the theory provides an explanation for the formation of groups by identical individuals. In the modern nuclear family there are, however, two types of individuals, adults and children. The nuclear family may not be an optimal size group if binding institutional restrictions determine its characteristic structure.

The theory of local public goods examines the properties of competitive equilibria under alternative constraints on group size. In an open model there is no constraint on population or group size. If all individuals are identical, the competitive equilibrium is Pareto efficient and there is equality within each group and between groups. In a closed model there is a population constraint. When there is free mobility between groups, the total population may be either too large or too small to support groups of optimal size. It is shown that the competitive equilibrium which is efficient can be unstable and that a stable equilibrium may not be Pareto efficient. When such a constraint exists, the second best solution may involve introducing institutional constraints on mobility between groups within the population. If it is assumed that individuals possess unequal endowments, the first order conditions identify the trade-off between efficiency in the formation of groups of optimal size and equity for the entire population. The binding constraint on population size is, in the neoclassical tradition, assumed to be apolitical in origin.

When identical adults form a household under the conditions characterising the open model, the household or family is a group of optimal size. Family members engage in trade and since there are no distortionary constraints there is equality between adults and between children within each family. There is also equality between families. Under these conditions, intergenerational trade within the family permits an efficient intertemporal allocation of resources and income equality.

If, however, there are binding constraints on household formation which, unlike the constraint implied by a fixed population, are institutional in origin, we do not have the same problem. If there are binding institutional constraints on household size, these determine the local public goods which the household can produce efficiently. When other groups, such as firms, are not subject to these constraints, the household is a relatively inefficient unit for the production of goods which require as inputs local public goods produced more efficiently by larger production units. In modern economies where individuals, upon leaving the market sector, must enter the household sector, these constraints act as constraints on entry into other groups. This encourages trade between households and other groups because households cannot produce all goods efficiently. In particular, it encourages trade between households and firms, despite a wage differential due to crowding in the household sector. Individuals in crowded market jobs cannot form a separate economy irrespective of their aggregate population size. This theory has implications for inequality among adults and among children.[13] The analysis of Chapters 4 and 5 examines the way in which constraints on household size determine directly the terms of trade between the market and household sectors and control indirectly the terms of trade between individuals in crowded and crowding market jobs.[14] With crowding inequality among adults, the assignment of children to the nuclear family in which they are supported by parents distorts the capital market so that crowding inequality can be perpetuated as described in section 3.3.

An important difference between family formation and the formation of other groups is that family size decisions determine aggregate population. The population models by Samuelson and others discussed above consider optimal population policy defined in terms of a rate of population growth which achieves maximum per capita welfare. If the welfare of all potential individuals is also considered, the population level which achieves the *total* welfare optimum does not necessarily coincide with the population level which achieves the *per capita* optimum. Meade (1955), in his discussion of optimal population, defines the optimal absolute level of population as that population where the total welfare gain on introducing the last individual is equal to the total welfare loss suffered by existing individuals.[15] He employs the concept of a 'welfare subsistence' level of real income: a level at which life is just enjoyable. If individuals have identical utility functions with diminishing marginal utility of income and there is a fixed factor, the optimum implies a population so large that everyone lives on a real income just sufficient to attain the welfare subsistence level. Clearly, an objection to a total welfare optimum at which everyone lives at subsistence is that a population size which allows a higher standard of living may be more acceptable.

The situation in which there are diminishing returns is represented by a local public goods model in which the local community is constrained to an above optimal population size in terms of per capita welfare. If we accept such a constraint as binding and choose a social welfare function which includes the welfare of potential individuals, the conflict between a total welfare optimum at which each individual lives at subsistence and a per capita welfare optimum is essentially a conflict over the choice of the 'correct' welfare subsistence level. Since the 'correct' welfare subsistence level depends upon whom society confers the right to choose it, the issue reduces to the choice of the social welfare function for existing individuals. If the right is conferred upon parents and they consider that their own incomes provide the acceptable subsistence level, they make family size decisions to coincide with a child quality which enables their children to earn the same lifetime incomes as they do. If the distribution of incomes among parents is accepted as the optimal income distribution, so also is the distribution of the so-called welfare subsistence level. If all parents choose to have the same number of children, the rate of population growth is the same for all income groups but the subsistence level varies. Cross section data would indicate a rise in the demand for child quality with parent income but no change in the demand for child quantity. From the life cycle perspective illustrated in Figure 3.1, each individual exactly reproduces itself at the full lifetime income and consumption expenditure of its parents. Thus we return to the fundamental issue which is whether inequality in parents' incomes, and therefore in the distribution of welfare subsistence levels, is due to given characteristics or to institutional constraints. With institutional inequality among parents, the dependence of children upon parents can, in this context, be seen to maintain differences in welfare 'subsistence' levels.

4

Work, leisure, institutional restrictions and income taxation

4.1 The specification of work and leisure

The definition of work and leisure used in interpreting the models presented here involves a fundamental point of departure from conventional theory. The theory of labour supply distinguishes between work and leisure as two demands for individual time. Labour supply is time allocated to work and wage income is the product of the hourly wage and hours supplied to work. The first order conditions for a utility maximum require that the individual equate the ratio of marginal utilities of leisure and work to the wage. In applications of this model, work and leisure are treated as the activities of institutionally recognised groups. Work is usually viewed as the supply of individual time to market activity, and leisure as the residual. For example, in interpreting the rules derived in optimal tax theory, work and leisure are taken to mean market and household activity respectively. In the theory of household production, the classification of household activity as leisure is rejected, and the activity choices of work and leisure are extended to include 'home work'.

It is proposed here that, technically, work is production for trade and leisure is production for own consumption. Individual activity, irrespective of any grouping of individuals, is production for trade to the extent that it involves social interaction and it is production for leisure to the extent that it is associated with own consumption. Labour supply refers to the supply of individual time to production for trade and wage income to the product of the hourly wage for production for trade (the trade wage) and labour supply. The individual maximizes utility which depends on the consumption of

47

goods obtained from trade and from production for own consumption. The first order conditions require that the ratio of marginal utilities of production for own consumption and for trade equal the wage.

Trade or social interaction occurs when individuals form groups. While the theory of local public goods explains the formation of an interacting group by uniformly endowed individuals as a response to scale economies, the two sector international trade model assumes constant returns to scale and attributes trade to non-uniform differences in the factor endowments of the trading partners forming a group. Irrespective of the theory chosen to explain group formation, individual activity in all groups is both production for trade and for consumption. This has implications for the identification of leisure, labour supply and wage income in a market–household economy. Neither household activity nor market activity can be classified solely as work or as leisure. In the market sector, examples of leisure are job status and satisfaction. Production for trade occurs within and between firms. Goods traded within the market sector include entertainment and travel on expense accounts, and luxury work environments. If individuals forming a household specialize in household activities and 'share' the household services they produce, there is a division of labour within the household as a production unit and there is production for trade. The trade is not monetised.

The household consisting of a single earner couple can be contrasted with the couple earning equal market sector incomes and sharing household chores. A dependent spouse produces household services which are purchased by the primary earner. The dependent spouse is paid a money wage income by the primary earner. If the status of the individual producing the same household services were classified as that of housekeeper instead of dependent spouse, the household services would be classified as market goods. In an economy of single earner couples there is thus a division of labour between dependent spouses producing household services and the single earners producing market goods. This division of labour between the household and market sectors might be attributed to scale economies, or it might be assumed that individuals in each sector have non-uniform differences in skills or in job preferences which result in specialization. If individuals are assumed homogeneous, the formation of the single earner household in which the market sector earner does not allocate time to 'home work' cannot be a response to scale economies within the household because there is no further division of labour: only the dependent spouse produces household services. In addition, the household sector does not achieve scale economies if there is no division of labour and trade between households. When there is trade between households the goods traded are classified as market goods. The organization of production and patterns of trade of the market and household sectors is thus asymmetric: in the market sector there is a division of labour and trade within and between firms whereas in the household sector there is only a division of labour and trade within the household in which individuals share in the production of household services. Thus, the formation of firms and the organization of market production can be explained in terms of scale economies, but the single earner household and the household sector as a whole cannot.

These observations have implications for interpreting the theory of household production.[1] Becker postulates that the household is a production unit and maximizes a household utility function. As a production unit the household combines market goods and household labour to produce household services in a way analogous to the firm's employment of labour and capital to produce market goods. The household chooses an allocation of time between 'market work' and 'home work' to maximize household utility which is a function of household services. There are, however, further similarities between the household and the firm not identified by Becker. There is no technical difference between labour supply decisions by individuals in the two production units. In the household sector a dependent spouse receives a money wage income for labour supply to the production of household services for trade just as in the firm individuals receive a money wage income for production for trade. In both sectors individuals allocate time to leisure.

When a distinction is made between 'home work' and 'home leisure',[2] the household utility function has three arguments: household services (produced by market goods and household labour), household leisure and market goods. Men are observed to choose between market work and home leisure and women to have three activity choices: market work, home work and home leisure. If a further distinction is made between market work and market leisure, one might postulate a household utility function with four arguments: market goods, household services, household leisure and market leisure. Such distinctions between activities are, however, based on the institutional location of work and leisure. In order to identify individual labour supply responses, the arguments of the household utility function must distinguish the traded goods and leisure of each individual. An implication of the use of purely institutional categories is that the disincentive effects of taxation cannot be identified. This problem is not recognised in the optimal tax literature where the wage income derived from the supply of labour to home work is not taken into account.

When the observed differences in activity choices of men and women reflect institutional constraints on job choices there are additional problems. Unless it is assumed that men and women possess non-uniform differences in their skills or preferences, household production theory fails to explain the assignment of one spouse to the household sector. Thus, if one spouse is assigned to home work, the theory is based on a given characteristics theory of employment segregation. When there is complete segregation which is attributed to sex differences in skills, we have trade between a dependent spouse employed in the household sector and the primary earner employed in the market sector under conditions characterising a simple international trade model.

The theory of crowding presented in Chapter 2 offers an explanation for employment segregation by sex which does not rely on non-uniform differences in skills. In section 4.2 all individuals are assumed to be innately identical and the role of women as secondary earners is explained in terms of constraints imposed on the market sector employment of women. Section 4.3 introduces constraints on household size and discusses implications for the structure of wages within the household and between the market and household sectors. In section 4.4 income taxation is identified as a selective tax on wage incomes. There is production for trade in the market and household sectors but income taxation taxes wage incomes only from trade between the market and household sectors. Moreover, income tax can be avoided by the formation of a household with a dependent spouse because the dependent spouse's wage income from the production of household services for trade is untaxed. Prior to Apps and Jones

(1980), the literature on the choice of the tax unit does not identify this form of wage income and this has led to policy conclusions based on an accounting error in the calculation of the true joint money incomes of couples. These issues are discussed in section 4.5. Optimal tax models which specify the untaxability of leisure as the only additional constraint on tax design do not take account of constraints imposed by the existing income tax systems in which some sources of wage income are untaxable. Apps and Jones specify the untaxability of the money wage income of the dependent spouse as an additional constraint on optimal tax design. The results are presented in section 4.6. An important feature of the models is that traded goods and leisure are not aggregated across individuals within a household. This allows the problem of identifying labour supply responses associated with the Becker type of household utility function to be avoided.

4.2   The crowding of women in the household sector

There are several ways in which constraints on the market sector employment of women may be imposed. The method examined in this section is the influence of social attitudes which engender the view that the proper role of women is full-time employment in the household sector as dependent spouses. These social attitudes may be analysed as a tax on production for own consumption in the market sector; that is, as a tax on leisure in the market sector. The effects of the 'tax' can be determined by the two sector model in Chapter 2. The tax crowds female labour in the household sector if it changes the sector employment ratio. In this case social attitudes are equivalent to a distortionary tariff on the entry of women into the market sector.

To assume that institutions can be used to control social attitudes so as to impose a constraint on the employment of women in the market sector, implies an event which gave men greater political power. The conditions associated with the event are of only historical interest. What matters is that men exercise their power through institutions which divide the economy into the market and household sectors and assign women to the household sector. The short run effect of crowding in the household sector is a fall in the relative price of household services and in the wage for household labour. Although wages differ between the household and the market sectors, there is no differential between the wage rate for males and females in the market sector. Inequality in market sector wages for men and women is explained as the long run effect of crowding. Women become less productive because they have lower incomes to invest in their human capital as a result of crowding in the household sector. When long run productivity differences between men and women are established in this way, females earn lower market sector wages than males, irrespective of whether market and household sector capital is homogeneous.

In the absence of institutional restrictions, differences in market sector wages for the same job do not necessarily reflect lifetime income inequality. It can be argued that human capital is sector specific and women choose employment in the household sector because they possess a comparative advantage in household production. Consequently they do not gain market sector specific human capital from learning on the job. Experience in the market sector can then be used as an explanatory variable for differences between male and female market sector wage rates.[3]

The analysis by Boskin (1974) recognises that social security provisions and joint income taxation impose tariffs on females entering market sector employment. Assuming human capital to be sector specific, Boskin points out that the tariffs induce females to specialise in the acquisition of household sector human capital and males in market sector human capital. The specialization reinforces segregation. The theory offers an explanation for unequal market sector wages for males and females who have different work experience. The tariffs must cause crowding in the household sector to create inequality between the sexes. When social attitudes also impose tariffs on wives taking market sector jobs, both induce long run productivity differences between the sexes irrespective of whether human capital is sector specific, because of circularity in the production of human capital. Pay differences can be justified by each individual employer because females entering the market sector from the household sector are less productive. Competition ensures that labour is paid its marginal value product, and the link between attitudes concerning the appropriate employment of women and the market sector wage inequality between males and females can be ignored.

Crowding in the household sector also explains the differences in factor intensities between the sectors. The household sector, with its lower level of per capita investment, becomes relatively labour intensive whereas the market sector, with its higher level of per capita investment, becomes more capital intensive. If institutional restrictions are considered unimportant, it may be suggested that the 'nature' of household services accounts for the relative labour intensity of the household sector and the 'nature' of market goods for the relative capital intensity of the market sector.[4] Comparisons between the technologies of the two sectors and between their division of labour indicate the extent to which the market sector is analogous to a developed economy and the household sector to a less developed economy. There is a contrast between the size and organisation of production units in the two sectors. The large number of separate households operating as independent decision making units, which in Becker (1965) are likened to small firms producing joint outputs for a small number of industries, have few similarities with the organisation of market firms and industries. Organisational and technological differences are also reflected in the spatial location of market and household activities. Housing is dispersed, whereas buildings and capital equipment for market production tend to be spatially concentrated. Constraints on household size can also account for these differences in the organisation of production in the two sectors and between male and female wage rates.

4.3   The effects of constraints on household size

The division of the economy into market and household sectors and the assignment of females to the household sector cannot crowd the household sector if it can produce the same goods as the market sector. Restrictions on the kinds of goods produced by the household are required. There are, however, no regulations specifying that market goods such as consumer durables cannot be produced in the household sector. Instead there are limitations on market sector activity which constrain most individuals (there may be exceptions in the higher wage market jobs) to household activity which is typically classed as 'home leisure'. Such constraints on the activities of firms cannot explain crowding in the household sector. There are constraints on which traded goods may be produced in firms. Individuals do not form firms to rear children because the product cannot be sold.[5] Aside from the public provision of education and of other services for children, the rearing of children outside the household sector is generally not permitted. The social conditioning of women to accept employment in household sector child rearing may account for some degree of crowding in the household sector. However, observation suggests that this constraint alone cannot fully explain the difference between average male and female market sector wages.[6] With modern medical technology and many families producing fewer children, the time taken for child rearing in the household sector is relatively short in comparison to an individual's lifetime. In addition, many services produced by females in the household sector are also produced in the market sector. Examples are prepared food, education, entertainment and recreation. Given these observations, household sector crowding is attributed here to indirect controls on household production imposed by constraints on household size.

It is proposed that the purpose of social attitudes is not just to crowd females in the household sector but to redress differences in what Becker (1973) refers to as the ability to identify 'own' children. In this skill men and women do differ innately. Women have a comparative advantage in identifying own children. In contrast, neither men nor women have a comparative advantage in nurturing children. Men cannot alone produce own children. For a man to acquire own children he must persuade a woman to agree to a relationship, such as marriage, which is sufficiently monogamous for him to identify own children. Becker (1973) postulates the production of own children as an explanation for marriage, or the formation of a household by one man and one woman, observing that 'Nothing distinguishes married households more from single households or from those with several members of the same sex than the presence, even indirectly, of children.' But the production of own children is a reason only for men to marry. Women can produce own children without marriage and, in a perfect capital market, child care costs can be financed from the child's future earnings. Women would not voluntarily enter marriage contracts unless they were at least indifferent. In the absence of institutional restrictions inducing marriage there would be equality between men and women or, if there was inequality, it would be in the opposite direction from that which we observe.[7]

Social attitudes could therefore be construed to have two objectives: the production of own children and higher wages for men. To these ends social attitudes encourage the formation of households by one man and one woman and discourage the market sector employment of women. The restriction on the market sector employment of women not only gains higher wages for men but also creates a wage structure which encourages marriage. In the absence of a perfect capital market, reducing the market sector wage for women discourages the production of own children by women out of marriage.

Social attitudes, in determining the size of the production unit in which women are employed, control the local public goods to which they have direct access. Under complete segregation there is no division of labour in the household sector. Such a constraint on the organization of household production reduces efficiency if there are scale economies for larger production units, as evidenced by the size of firms which produce substitutes for household services, including child care. The household is most constrained in producing those goods whose efficient production requires large scale production plants. In contrast, Becker (1973) believes the household to be an optimal size production unit. He fails to note that unless individuals share household production there is no division of labour in the household as a production unit. Instead he suggests 'diminishing returns to scale' from adding persons (adults) to a household having one man and one woman.

The effect of a binding constraint on household size is to reduce the substitutability between market goods and household services in household production (Becker's complementarity between own time and market goods in household production). This introduces a production asymmetry between sectors. In the market sector there are market goods which are close substitutes for household services in the production of capital and, in turn, in the production of market goods. But in the household sector, because of constraints on household size, household services are not close substitutes for market goods. This causes the demand for market goods as factors of household production to be inelastic when the demand for household services as factors of market production is relatively elastic. The relationship between demand elasticities can, for the special case where group 1 and group 2 are the same size and institutional restrictions cause employment segregation but not inequality, be stated as

$$|\varepsilon_y^1| > |\varepsilon_x^2| \tag{4.1}$$

where ε_y^1 denotes the elasticity of demand for household services by a market sector worker, given by $y_p^1 \dfrac{p}{y^1} - 1$, $\cdot \varepsilon_x^2$ denotes the elasticity of demand for market goods by a household sector worker, given by $x_p^2 \dfrac{p}{x^2}$.

In a two sector closed economy with employment segregation, a change in a group's demand elasticity is associated with a corresponding change, opposite in direction, in the group's supply elasticity. The relation in (4.1) therefore implies that, in terms of absolute values, the supply elasticity exceeds the demand elasticity for market goods. Thus, institutional constraints on the employment of women in the household sector control elasticities relevant in determining the price effects of crowding and, as we shall see in Chapter 5, the incidence of income taxation as a tax on trade between the two sectors.

This section has focused on social attitudes as an explanation for the crowding of women in the household sector. We shall now consider how the structure of taxation also encourages the formation of households and can contribute further to the crowding of women in household production.

4.4   The structure of income taxation

The theory of optimal taxation focuses on second best solutions to tax design when leisure is untaxable and is seen to take account of work disincentive effects which were ignored in the minimum sacrifice theory.[8] But when work is defined as production for trade, it can be observed that existing tax systems fail to tax various sources of wage income as well as leisure.[9] Wage income from trade within and between firms in the market sector is untaxed. In-kind wage income derived from a division of labour and trade within the household is untaxed and the money wage income earned by a dependent spouse for labour supply to the production of household services for trade is untaxed. Optimal tax models do not necessarily take account of the relevant effects of taxation on work effort if currently untaxed forms of wage income cannot, for whatever reason, be included in the tax base.

Taxes on wage incomes can be avoided by switching to leisure or to activity in groups within which production for trade is untaxed. An example of the latter is switching from the market production of household services as a housekeeper to the production of the same services as a dependent spouse. Income taxation can, in general, be avoided by

(i) forming firms to produce goods for trade within and between firms;
(ii) forming households (including adults and children) to produce goods for trade within the household; and
(iii) becoming a dependent of a market sector earner

In response to such a tax structure individuals form only two kinds of production units to produce for trade: firms and households. If there were no restrictions on the activities of firms, there would be no reason for household production. All goods would be produced by firms in the market sector, and tax would be avoided since there is no tax on trade between firms. To explain household production we require that individuals be assigned to the household sector either because of their given characteristics or because of institutional reasons.

When all individuals are required to perform some activities in the household sector for which there are no perfect substitutes in the market sector, they may form households either individually or collectively, with economies of scale the incentive for the latter. Tax avoidance by becoming partly or fully dependent on a market sector earner would be practised only in couples where the individuals earn unequal market sector incomes either because they are innately different or because they face different constraints on entry into market sector jobs. Once the wage and employment segregation effects of constraints on the market sector employment of women are established, the tax system reinforces those effects. A relatively small tax advantage for becoming a dependent spouse can provide a sufficient incentive to do so if women are crowded in low wage market jobs.

It is easy to see that direct taxes on market sector wage incomes and indirect taxes on market goods are taxes on trade between the market and household sectors. It is perhaps less obvious that the corporation tax is the same type of trade tax. Although widely treated as a tax on income from corporate capital, the corporation tax and the tax on corporate dividends are taxes on trade between the market and household sectors. Both can be avoided by retaining and investing corporate profits for consumption within the corporation. When all costs of market production, including true depreciation, can be offset against total revenue, factors employed in market production for consumption within the sector are untaxed. The factors are subject to tax if factor incomes are transferred to the household sector in which case the tax is on trade between the two sectors. Under a separate entity system of corporation tax, distributed profits are subject to this trade taxation twice, first at the corporate level and then at the personal income tax level. Under a fully integrated system, dividend payments are subject to the trade tax once, as are interest payments to savings held in bank deposits or the component of housing rental incomes subject to income tax.

Factors of household production only escape taxation provided they are produced within the household. Factors of market production escape taxation if they are produced within the market sector. Additional differences in the tax treatment of households and firms would be introduced by a tax on imputed incomes from household labour or capital (such as a tax on an imputed rent for owner occupied housing). A tax on imputed household income would include some component of leisure, and leisure is not taxed in the firm. If leisure in the firm, including job status, were also taxed, symmetrical treatment with respect to leisure would be restored. But leisure cannot be taxed directly and various sources of wage income will inevitably remain untaxed. In any case, broadening the tax base does not return us to a first best tax problem in the presence of institutional constraints causing inequality.

4.5   The tax unit

In the choice of the tax unit, the criteria of equal taxation of couples with equal money resources, tax neutrality with respect to marriage and progressivity in the rate of tax on money are generally considered to be conflicting. Under a progressive income tax, equal taxation of couples requires that they be considered as an economic unit, with taxes based on the amount of joint income, not on the distribution of income between spouses. However, neutrality requires that there should be no penalty for marital status. The 'conflict' is illustrated by comparing single earner and two earner couples. Consider a single earner couple with a market sector wage income of $20,000 and a two earner couple with each spouse earning a market sector wage income of $10,000. Equal taxation is said to require that the two couples pay the same amount of tax because they 'share' incomes whereas neutrality under a progressive tax requires the individual earning the $20,000 to pay more tax than the two spouses each earning $10,000. It is concluded that horizontal equity between couples calls for joint taxation and neutrality for individual taxation. The conclusion ignores the untaxed money wage income of the dependent spouse. 'Sharing' or 'pooling' of resources can be interpreted as the imputation of a wage income for a fully or partly dependent spouse equal to half the after-tax differential between the market sector incomes of spouses. If this amounts to $14,000 for the single earner couple, the dependent spouse earns $7,000. The true joint money income of the single earner couple is $27,000. The joint money income of the two earner couple where there is no sharing is $20,000. The criteria are not necessarily conflicting.

It is also considered that the labour supply decision of each spouse should be independent of the after-tax income of the other spouse; that the marginal rate of tax payable by one spouse should not affect the labour supply decision of the other. This criterion is violated by joint taxation, since under joint taxation the secondary earner faces the same marginal tax rate as the primary earner. The efficiency loss caused by different labour supply elasticities of spouses increases as the wage elasticity of the secondary earner increases.[10] Although it is recognised that joint taxation may cause a considerable efficiency loss, its supporters argue that a trade-off is required between the efficiency loss and the supposed equity advantage of equal taxation under joint taxation. But conventional joint taxation does not achieve equal taxation of couples with the same true money resources because the wage income of the dependent spouse is untaxed. Instead, it taxes couples with the same true money resources, but different distributions of market sector incomes, more unequally than a conventional individual basis of tax and simultaneously increases the efficiency cost of taxation.[11]

Discussions of the tax unit also express a concern for equity between individuals living alone and the couple who, by a division of labour and sharing household expenditures, can live more cheaply than one. On the basis of this criterion, different rate schedules for single individuals and couples are frequently justified. But a tax on wage incomes is a tax on trade. Provided there are no institutional reasons for group formation, trade between identical individuals occurs in response to scale economies from forming trading groups. Under this condition, it is unnecessary to treat scale economies as an additional consideration in the choice of the tax unit.

The view that the above criteria are relevant and some are necessarily conflicting reveals fundamental problems in discussions of the choice of the tax unit. In particular, the view is based on the misspecification of work and leisure in the theory of labour supply. This has led to support for tax structures designed to tax families with two equal market sector earners more heavily than single or primary earner families with the same true money resources. Since secondary earners are most commonly women, joint taxation acts as a tariff on the entry of women into the market sector and in this way reinforces the effects of social attitudes discouraging women from market sector employment.

The disadvantage for two earner couples of a conventional individual basis of tax increases as the differential in their market sector incomes declines. This is because the size of the accounting error in the calculation of joint incomes increases. Table 4.1 shows the size of the accounting error for three couples when dependent spouses are paid a wage income equal to half the after-tax differential in market sector incomes. Couple 1 consists of a single earner on $20,000 and a fully dependent spouse; couple 2 consists of a primary earner on $15,000 and a secondary earner on $5,000; and couple 3 are two market sector earners each with a market sector wage income of $10,000. A comparison between the figures in columns 3 and 5 indicates the size of the error made in the conventional calculation of the aggregate money incomes of spouses when the rate of tax on taxable incomes is 0.3 and a lump sum transfer of $500 is paid to all individuals. The difference between the figures in columns 4 and 6 shows the income which is untaxed when couples can split incomes.

Columns 7 and 8 contrast figures for average rates of tax on true joint incomes and on conventionally defined joint incomes under a conventional individual basis of tax.[12] The figures show that the average rate of tax on the true joint money resources of the couples is overstated when one spouse is fully or partly dependent. Notice that the tax is regressive on true joint incomes. This illustrates the way in which a nominally progressive tax can be regressive, especially when two earner couples predominate at the lower end of the distribution of individual incomes.

The same errors underlie the treatment of marriage as a partnership. Treating marriage as a partnership assumes that spouses produce only for monetised trade outside the group. In marriage, the dependent spouse produces for monetised trade. The omission of the wage income of the dependent spouse is also found in the calculation of joint investment incomes. Meade (1978), for example, suggests that a family in which each spouse has an investment income of $5,000 be taxed the same amount as a family where one spouse has an investment income of $10,000 and shares it with the other spouse. If spouses equally share money resources and tax on $10,000 investment income is, say, $3,000, this implies additional untaxed wage income of $3,500 for the spouse earning no investment income.

The figures in Table 4.1 indicate that a proportional income tax with no exemptions does not avoid the problems which arise from the untaxability of the money wage income of a dependent spouse. A proportional income tax on individual market sector incomes is not neutral with respect to marriage. It is only thought to be neutral because the conventional individual basis of tax is assumed to be a true individual basis. It is important to recognise that four bases of tax can be distinguished:

(i) true individual taxation
(ii) conventional individual taxation
(iii) true joint taxation
(iv) conventional joint taxation

It is well recognised that a single earner household is advantaged because the imputed value of the work of the spouse who stays at home is not taxed, and that a two earner household is disadvantaged by additional costs associated with the second spouse going out to work. It is sometimes considered that this problem would be resolved if the tax base could be broadened to include an imputed value for the dependent spouse's labour time or if deductions were allowed for costs associated with the second spouse going out to work. However, any proposals to tax the imputed value of the dependent spouse's labour may be criticised because the imputation of a wage income for a dependent spouse based on the spouse's market sector opportunity wage assumes that labour supply is observable. This assumption is rejected in optimal tax theory. A deduction for the full additional cost of a second earner is equivalent to a deduction for the imputed value of household services a spouse would produce if dependent.

Table 4.1 Money incomes of couples with 'sharing' of market sector wage incomes

	Market sector money income		True money income		Market sector money income		Average rate of tax using true money income	Average rate of tax using market sector income
	Spouse A	Spouse B	$ Joint (income aggregation)	$ Average (income splitting)	$ Joint (income aggregation)	$ Average (income splitting)		
	1	2	3	4	5	6	7	8
Couple 1	20,000	0	27,000	13,500	20,000	10,000	0.19	0.25
Couple 2	15,000	5,000	23,500	11,750	20,000	10,000	0.21	0.25
Couple 3	10,000	10,000	20,000	10,000	20,000	10,000	0.25	0.25

Thus, a proposal of this kind suggests a deduction for the opportunity cost of leisure to the extent that a part of the cost of working in the market sector is foregone production of household services for own consumption by a dependent spouse. Notice that the two kinds of proposals treat the issue as a direct and indirect tax problem respectively.[13]

In contrast to the idea of taxing an imputed value for the dependent spouse's work at home, proponents of joint taxation, in their imputation of the share of the primary earner's money resources paid to a dependent spouse, do not imply that labour supply is observable or that leisure in any form should be taxed. In assigning a share of the primary earner's money income to a dependent spouse it is, however, assumed that the wage income of a dependent spouse is observable. In contrast to leisure, which is untaxable because it is unobservable, the dependent spouse's wage income is untaxed for institutional reasons alone.

4.6 The optimal tax structure with the wage income of the dependent spouse untaxable

This section presents results from Apps and Jones (1980) for an optimal linear income tax when the wage income of the dependent spouse is untaxable. The models imply that the untaxability of other forms of wage income, including wage income from non-monetised trade within the household and monetised trade within the market sector, does not impose additional constraints. It is also assumed that the dependent spouse's wage income is observable and is a proportion, γ, of the wage income of the primary earner. This corresponds to the accepted view that spouses 'share' money resources. The purpose of the analysis is to examine the policy implications of the untaxability of the wage income of dependent spouses subject to standard assumptions of tax theory. Limiting the analysis in this way should not be interpreted to imply that the wage income of a dependent spouse is, in fact, easily observable.

We can consider the results of a simple model which allows the optimal linear income tax structure for an economy of single earner couples to be compared with that for an economy of single individuals

or of two earner couples who do not share incomes. The tax parameters are α, the lump sum transfer, and β, the marginal tax rate.
Individual utility depends on the consumption of a composite commodity, x, obtained from trade and labour supply, l, which can be
interpreted as foregone own consumption. There are two groups: group 1
represents actual or potential primary earner spouses (males) who work
only in the market sector and group 2 represents actual or potential
secondary earner spouses (females) who work either in the market sector
or in the household sector as dependent spouses. Individuals within each
group have identical utility functions which can be written as

$$u^1 = u^1(x^1, l^1), \; u^2 = u^2(x^2, l^2) \qquad u_1^1, u_1^2 > 0; u_2^1, u_2^2 < 0$$

where superscripts 1 and 2 refer to a group 1 individual and a group 2
individual, respectively.[14] Subscripts denote partial derivatives.

The after-tax budget constraint for a group 1 individual is given by

$$x^1 = \alpha + (1 - \beta)wl^1$$

where w is the before-tax wage. The budget constraint for a group 2
individual when taxed in the market sector is given by

$$x^2 = \alpha + (1 - \beta)w^*l^2$$

and when untaxed as a dependent spouse by

$$x^2 = w^*l^2$$

where w^* is the before-tax wage.[15]

Conventional formulations of the optimal tax problem do not take
account of institutional links between the wage rates of different groups. In
particular, an institutional relationship between male and female wages is
not introduced. A purpose of the tax incidence analyses in Chapters 5 and
6 is to identify second round effects when institutional constraints influence the structure of relative wages. However, for the present analysis a link
between the wage rates of groups 1 and 2 is indicated simply by setting

$$w^*l^2 = \gamma(\alpha, \beta, w^*(l^2(\alpha, \beta)))wl^1$$

When x^2 represents the wage income of a dependent spouse, $\gamma(.)$ is the
proportion of the market sector earner's wage income used to purchase
household services. Alternatively, when x^2 denotes the wage income of a
female market sector earner, $\gamma(.)$ represents the institutional relationship

between male and female wages throughout the economy. This relationship does not impose inequality by sex and, for consistency with standard assumptions of tax theory, equality between spouses can be assumed in interpreting the results for the optimal tax parameters.

The results can be derived using the procedure in Sheshinski (1972) or in Dixit and Sandmo (1977). Following Sheshinski (1972), the first order conditions yield

$$
\beta = \begin{cases}
\dfrac{\displaystyle\int_0^\infty \left\{ 1 - \dfrac{\mu^1}{\lambda} - \dfrac{\mu^2}{\lambda}\left(1 + w\hat{l}^1\dfrac{\partial \hat{l}^1}{\partial \alpha} + \gamma w\dfrac{\partial \hat{l}^1}{\partial \alpha}\right) \right\} f(w)\,dw}{\displaystyle\int_0^\infty \left\{ w\dfrac{\partial \hat{l}^1}{\partial \alpha} + \dfrac{\partial \hat{w}^*\hat{l}^2}{\partial \alpha} - \dfrac{\mu^2}{\lambda}\left(w\hat{l}^1\dfrac{\partial \gamma}{\partial \alpha} + \gamma w\dfrac{\partial \hat{l}^1}{\partial \alpha}\right) \right\} f(w)\,dw} \\[3em]
\dfrac{\displaystyle\int_0^\infty \left\{ \left(\dfrac{\mu^1}{\lambda}-1\right)w\hat{l}^1 + \left(\dfrac{\mu^2}{\lambda}-1\right)\hat{w}^*\hat{l}^2 - \dfrac{\mu^2}{\lambda}\left(w\hat{l}^1\dfrac{\partial \gamma}{\partial \beta} + \gamma w\dfrac{\partial \hat{l}^1}{\partial \beta}\right) \right\} f(w)\,dw}{\displaystyle\int_0^\infty \left\{ w\dfrac{\partial \hat{l}^1}{\partial \beta} + \dfrac{\partial \hat{w}^*\hat{l}^2}{\partial \beta} - \dfrac{\mu^2}{\lambda}\left(w\hat{l}^1\dfrac{\partial \gamma}{\partial \beta} + \gamma w\dfrac{\partial \hat{l}^1}{\partial \beta}\right) \right\} f(w)\,dw}
\end{cases}
$$

where α and β are the optimal tax parameters when all wage incomes are taxed. In contrast,

$$
\tilde{\beta} = \begin{cases}
\dfrac{\displaystyle\int_0^\infty \left\{ 1 - \dfrac{\mu^1}{\lambda} - \dfrac{\mu^2}{\lambda}\left(w\hat{l}^1\dfrac{\partial \gamma}{\partial \tilde{\alpha}} + \gamma w\dfrac{\partial \hat{l}^1}{\partial \tilde{\alpha}}\right) \right\} f(w)\,dw}{\displaystyle\int_0^\infty w\dfrac{\partial \hat{l}^1}{\partial \tilde{\alpha}} f(w)\,dw} \\[3em]
\dfrac{\displaystyle\int_0^\infty \left(\dfrac{\mu^1}{\lambda}-1\right)w\hat{l}^1 - \dfrac{\mu^2}{\lambda}\left(w\hat{l}^1\dfrac{\partial \gamma}{\partial \tilde{\beta}} + \partial w\dfrac{\partial \hat{l}^1}{\partial \tilde{\beta}}\right) f(w)\,dw}{\displaystyle\int_0^\infty w\dfrac{\partial \hat{l}^1}{\partial \tilde{\beta}} f(w)\,dw}
\end{cases}
$$

where $\tilde{\alpha}$ and $\tilde{\beta}$ are the optimal tax parameters when the wage incomes of dependent spouses are untaxed. λ is the social marginal utility of tax revenue. μ^1 and μ^2 are the marginal utilities of income and $\hat{l}^1$ and $\hat{l}^2$ the optimal labour supplies of individuals 1 and 2, respectively. It is assumed that leisure is a normal good and that labour supply is a non-decreasing function of the net wage rate; that is

$$\frac{\partial \hat{l}}{\partial (1 - \beta)} \geqq 0 \tag{4.2}$$

This excludes a decrease in wage income with an increase in the wage – a condition which would preclude redistribution by a progressive income tax.

The results show that, except under special conditions, the optimal tax structure tends to be more progressive when the wage income of dependent spouses cannot be taxed directly by government. If government has the option of varying the marginal tax rate by household composition, the optimal rate for individuals forming two earner couples is likely to be lower than that for single earner couples, with the differential in optimal rates increasing as single earner couples tend to be higher wage. In contrast to the optimal tax structure suggested by these results, countries which adopt different rate schedules depending on marital status apply the schedule with the higher marginal tax rates not just to couples with dependent spouses but to two earner couples with no dependent spouse. Such tax systems can be criticised on both equity and efficiency grounds for imposing higher taxes on two earner couples than on single earner couples with the same true money resources.

When the tax system is constrained to a single linear rate and single lump sum transfer in an economy of individuals, of two earner couples and of single earner couples, the optimal tax structure is likely to be more progressive than when all true wage incomes are taxable. Increased progressivity offsets to some extent the tendency towards regressivity which is introduced by the untaxability of the dependent spouse's wage income as indicated by the average tax rates on true incomes in Table 4.1. Indeed, unless the tax is sufficiently progressive, a two earner couple can pay more tax than a single earner couple with a higher true money income. In general, there is a trade-off in tax design between the efficiency cost of tax avoidance by one spouse becoming dependent and the equity gain from taxing indirectly the wage income of the dependent spouse, and the equity gain increases as the dependent spouse tends to be a luxury. These results imply that switching to an individual basis of tax modified to tax dependent spouses indirectly, would improve efficiency and reduce inequality caused by institutional crowding and reinforced by existing tax systems.

5

The incidence of income taxation as a tax on trade

5.1 Income taxation as a tax on trade between the market and household sectors

When institutional restrictions divide the population into two groups and assign one group to the household sector and the other to the market sector, we observe two labour forces which specialize and trade. They are analogous to two trading countries. This situation arises within an economy of single earner couples where the single earner does not allocate time to 'home work'. Under the current structure of direct taxation the wage income of the dependent spouse is untaxed and the wage income of the single earner is taxed. Under indirect taxation, traded household goods are untaxed but market goods traded with the household are taxed. Indirect taxation is like a tax on market sector exports to the household sector or a tariff on household sector imports of market goods. Both direct and indirect taxes can be treated as a tax on trade between the two sectors.

This chapter presents an analysis of the distribution of the burden of taxation between the market and household sectors when employment in each sector is fixed by institutional constraints. Section 5.2 presents a general model for the incidence of a tax on trade between two sectors with fixed labour forces in a closed economy. All individuals are assumed to be innately homogeneous in abilities and tastes. Each individual produces for external trade or for consumption. Thus each individual produces only for trade between the two sectors; trade within each sector is ignored. Production functions are circular.

The results can be interpreted in a number of contexts. Section 5.3 discusses the implications of the results for the distribution of the

67

burden of income taxation between couples or spouses forming single earner households. When the single earner is male and the dependent spouse female, the conclusions hold for the distribution of the burden of income taxation between men and women. Section 5.4 applies the model to the analysis of tax incidence when all individuals are, for institutional reasons, required to allocate some time to the household sector. When there are institutional limits on the kinds of activities an individual can perform in the market sector, the individual may purchase market goods, which are more efficiently produced in firms, for its household activity. In other words, each individual may trade market and household goods. This trade is also taxed under income taxation.

Although all individuals in the market sector produce for consumption to some extent, it can be observed that opportunities for consumption on the job differ between wage classes. Section 5.5 examines the implications for the distribution of the burden of income taxation among families when market sector labour employed in lower wage jobs has limited status and few opportunities for on-the-job consumption. Low wage market labour and household labour are similarly restricted in consumption opportunities. In section 5.6 the conclusions concerning the distribution of tax burdens within and between households are contrasted with the outcomes which are possible under the usual assumptions of optimal tax theory. A re-interpretation of rules for optimal taxation, based on the definition of work as production for trade and leisure as production for own consumption in the market and household sectors, is suggested. Section 5.7 comments on the characteristics of the optimal tax structure when, in addition to untaxed leisure, there are untaxed wage incomes derived from production for trade within the market sector and within the household. Section 5.8 concludes with a note on the interpretation of labour supply responses.

For the purpose of the trade tax analysis of income taxation, the assignment of particular groups to household production is simply taken as given. The previous chapter attributed the predominance of women in the household sector to institutional constraints imposed by social attitudes and the tax structure. There are many other groups also assigned to the household sector for institutional reasons. Children, the retired and the unemployed are examples. These groups typically consist of less powerful individuals in society and the results of the trade tax model, although interpreted here only for selected contexts, have implications for the incidence of income taxation on these groups as well. The model can also be applied to the analysis of the incidence of tariffs and taxes on trade between 'developed' and 'developing' economies.[1]

5.2 The incidence of a tax on trade

As in the models presented in Chapter 2, we let sector 1 producing good X represent market production and sector 2 producing good Y, household production. Although individuals are innately identical, they can be distinguished on the basis of non-economic characteristics and are divided into two groups accordingly. Let n denote the number of individuals in group 1 and m the number of individuals in group 2.

Institutional restrictions are introduced which fix employment in each sector by requiring individuals in group 1 to work only in sector 1 and individuals in group 2 to work only in sector 2. Prior to the restrictions, we set

$$p = w = 1 \tag{5.1}$$

If the restrictions do not alter the sector employment ratio they cause segregation but not inequality ($k^1 = k^2$). If the restrictions crowd sector 2, in the short run we have

$$p = w > 1 \tag{5.2}$$

The change in the sector employment ratio is positive. There is segregation and inequality ($k^1 \neq k^2$).

Given employment segregation and equality (5.1) or inequality (5.2), we introduce a tax on trade between the two sectors. The tax, t, is imposed on the price of good X facing sector 2. The equilibrium condition in (2.5) becomes

$$x^1(p, \, px) + \gamma x^2(p + t, \, y) = x$$

Assuming a unique interior solution for p and substituting for $\dfrac{\partial x}{\partial p}$, we obtain

$$\frac{\partial p}{\partial t} = \frac{-x_p^2 - x_y^2 \dfrac{\partial y}{\partial p}}{x_p^2 + x_y^2 \dfrac{\partial y}{\partial p} - \dfrac{x^2}{y^1}\left(y_p^1 + y_{px}^1 \dfrac{\partial px}{\partial p}\right) + \dfrac{x^2}{p}} \tag{5.3}$$

as t approaches zero. Evaluating at $\dfrac{\partial y}{\partial p}, \dfrac{\partial px}{\partial p} = 0$, the result in (5.3) reduces to

$$\frac{\partial p}{\partial t} = \frac{-1}{1 - \dfrac{\varepsilon_y^1}{\varepsilon_x^2}} \tag{5.4}$$

where $\varepsilon_y^1 = y_p^1 \dfrac{P}{y^1} - 1, \; \varepsilon_x^2 = x_p^2 \dfrac{P}{x^2}$.

If we assume that the utility function is locally linear, the burden of tax on an individual can be treated in terms of the change in the individual's capital ownership due to the tax.[2] Let β^1 and β^2 denote the burdens for representative individuals in group 1 and group 2, respectively. The ratio of burdens is given by

$$\frac{\dfrac{\partial \beta^1}{\partial t}}{\dfrac{\partial \beta^2}{\partial t}} = \frac{y_k \dfrac{\partial x}{\partial p}\dfrac{\partial p}{\partial t}}{x_k \dfrac{\partial y}{\partial p}\left(\dfrac{\partial p}{\partial t} + 1\right)} \gtreqless 1$$

as

$$\frac{\partial p}{\partial t} \lesseqgtr \frac{-1}{1 + \dfrac{y^1}{px^2}\dfrac{k^1}{k^2}}$$

or, by substitution from the trade relation in (2.9), as[3]

$$\frac{\partial p}{\partial t} \lesseqgtr \frac{-1}{1 + \gamma \dfrac{k^1}{k^2}} \tag{5.5}$$

or, from (5.4), as

$$\frac{|\varepsilon_y^1|}{|\varepsilon_x^2|} \lesseqgtr \gamma \frac{k^1}{k^2} \tag{5.6}$$

as t approaches zero.

If there is equality $(k^1 = k^2)$ prior to the introduction of the tax, then

$$\frac{\dfrac{\partial \beta^1}{\partial t}}{\dfrac{\partial \beta^2}{\partial t}} \gtrless 1$$

as

$$|\varepsilon_y^1| \lessgtr \gamma |\varepsilon_x^2| \tag{5.7}$$

This result shows that the incidence of an increment in the trade tax is determined by the relative absolute values of individual elasticities of demand for the foreign goods, weighted by the employment ratio. When there is inequality, it is necessary to weight elasticities by the ratio of capital ownership (k^1/k^2) to determine the incidence of the tax. The result has the general interpretation that the burden of tax on a group increases as the group's demand for the foreign good becomes more inelastic. The result can also be interpreted in terms of supply and demand elasticities for the foreign good. The relative burden on a group becomes greater as the supply elasticity of the foreign good exceeds the absolute value of the group's demand elasticity. Introducing the second round effects shown in the relationship in (5.3) modifies the tax incidence result in quantitative terms, but not the direction of the result.

5.3   The incidence of income taxation in an economy of single earner households

In an economy of single earner households with female dependent spouses, there is employment segregation into the market and house-hold sectors on the basis of sex. Under conventional systems of income taxation, the dependent spouse does not pay tax on wage income but the market sector earner does. The tax on the market sector earner's wage income is a tax on trade between the market and household sectors. The trade occurs between men and women and so the distribution of the tax burden between the market and household sectors corresponds to the distribution between men and women. If sector 1 represents the market sector and sector 2 the household

sector, the results of the previous model can be used to determine the
distribution of the tax burden by sex. If we assume the number of men
and women is equal, the distribution of the burden of an increment in
tax, ignoring second round effects, is given by

$$\frac{\dfrac{\partial \beta^1}{\partial t}}{\dfrac{\partial \beta^2}{\partial t}} \gtrless 1$$

as

$$\frac{\partial p}{\partial t} \gtrless \frac{-1}{1 + \dfrac{k^1}{k^2}}$$

or, from (5.6), as

$$\frac{|\varepsilon_y^1|}{|\varepsilon_x^2|} \lessgtr \frac{k^1}{k^2}$$

or, if there is equality, as

$$|\varepsilon_y^1| \lessgtr |\varepsilon_x^2|$$

which yields

$$\frac{\partial p}{\partial t} \gtrless -\frac{1}{2}$$

Thus, the distribution of the burden of an increment in income
taxation depends on the relationship between demand elasticities. If
there is equality before the change in tax the burden is equally
distributed when demand elasticities are equal. Despite restrictions on
the employment of women causing segregation and inequality, there is
no apriori reason to expect a relationship between elasticities which
would result in a greater proportional burden falling on either group.
In particular, to obtain the result that the tax is regressive, it is
necessary to introduce conditions which have different effects on the
demand elasticities of the two sectors.

In Chapter 4 it was argued that institutional constraints on household size, together with constraints on the entry of women into the
market sector, cause demand elasticities to diverge. The consequent

relationship between demand elasticities indicated in (4.1) implies

$$|\varepsilon_y^1| > \frac{k^1}{k^2} |\varepsilon_x^2|$$

It follows that

$$\frac{\partial p}{\partial t} > \frac{-1}{1 + \dfrac{k^1}{k^2}}$$

Under this condition the tax is regressive since the household sector is the low wage sector. If the demand for market goods is sufficiently inelastic, the absolute burden of the tax can be greater on the household sector. If this occurs, additional income taxation increases inequality between the market and household sectors and, therefore, between men and women: women effectively pay a greater share of the tax than men. Second round effects can reduce the burden on women and increase the burden on men, but the tax remains regressive.

In Chapter 4 social attitudes were identified as a method for assigning women to the household sector and joint taxation was shown to reinforce social attitudes. The result that the tax is regressive depends crucially on women being restricted to the household sector. Income taxation can increase inequality between the sexes only if women remain limited to employment in the household. If social attitudes alter or if tax reforms replace joint taxation by a true individual basis of taxation, income taxation may no longer exacerbate inequality between men and women.

5.4 The incidence of income taxation with constraints on the activities of firms

The high concentration of males as primary or single earners indicates that there is extensive market-household employment segregation by sex and, therefore, that a large part of trade between the market and household sectors takes place between men and women. Thus, if the conclusion of the previous section is correct, the burden of increments in income taxation is largely shifted to women. An obvious objection to the result is that the analysis ignores taxed transfers of market goods to the household sector which do not involve trade between men and women. It can be observed that individuals employed in the market sector purchase market goods for use in their own household activities. These transfers involve taxed trade between production units – firms and households – but not between individuals.[4]

The observation that the tax is not always avoided can be explained by additional constraints. Examples are constraints on the kinds of activities which can be performed in the market sector discussed in Chapter 4. Alternatively, hours of employment in the market sector might be limited (an eight hour day with no overtime). When an individual cannot entirely avoid household production, market goods are likely to be transferred to the household sector for own use despite the tax. For an analysis of the incidence of a tax on these transfers, an individual employed in the market sector can be treated as two individuals: as an individual in group 1 when employed in the market sector and as an individual in group 2 when employed in the household sector, where the two individuals trade market goods for household services. The results of the trade tax analysis in section 5.3 apply: a proportionally greater burden of tax falls on the individual when restricted to the household sector. The plausibility of this crowding and tax incidence theory for an individual employed in both sectors is supported by the results of empirical research on time values which indicate that the value of an individual's time in the market sector is higher than the value of the same individual's time in the household sector.

The kinds of activities upon which there are frequently limits in the market sector are those traditionally considered as leisure, such as eating, sleeping, travel and various forms of entertainment. However, the extent to which these are excluded from the market sector can be observed to vary with job position and status. The distribution of the burden of income taxation on household incomes will now be considered under the assumption that opportunities for on-the-job consumption in the market sector increase with the wage.

5.5 The incidence of income taxation on household incomes

To this point it has been assumed that there is a single wage rate within each sector. We shall now introduce wage classes within the two sectors. For simplicity, we can consider just two classes. In the market sector there is a high wage crowding occupation, 1A, and a low wage crowded occupation, 1B. Females are employed only in the household sector. Because of institutional restrictions, individuals of opposite sex form single earner households. Thus trade between the market and household sectors occurs between the male and the female within each household. We assume each male is limited to employing one dependent spouse (a man can take only one wife) and that this imposes a binding constraint on the supply of labour to employment as dependent spouses. Consequently, crowding inequality between males in the market sector produces corresponding inequality between females because the wage for a dependent spouse is determined solely by trade between the two individuals forming a household. The higher the wage earned by the male in the market sector, the higher the wage of his dependent spouse.

In addition to these wage inequalities between households, suppose there are greater opportunities for consumption on-the-job in occupation 1A because it is high status, the nature of the work is interesting, and expense accounts are provided for travel, entertainment and the purchase of other goods for consumption within the market sector. In contrast, suppose that occupation 1B has low status (though more than the crowded household sector), that the work is tedious and that the environment offers few opportunities for on-the-job consumption. Under these conditions, market goods and household services are close substitutes for members of the high wage occupation. They can switch easily from household services to untaxed consumption of market goods within the firm. However, market goods and household services are not close substitutes for members of the low wage occupation. Thus, we have

$$|\varepsilon_y^{1A}| > |\varepsilon_y^{1B}|$$

where ε_y^{1A} is the elasticity of demand for household services by a male employed in high wage occupation $1A$ and ε_y^{1B} is the elasticity of demand for household services by a male employed in low wage occupation $1B$. Applying the trade tax model we can conclude that a greater burden of tax is shifted by males employed in high wage occupation $1A$.

When trade between occupations $1A$ and $1B$ is introduced and dependent spouses receive wage incomes which they use to purchase goods produced by both market sector occupations, it is easy to see that low wage households may ultimately bear the greater burden of tax. Suppose that occupation $1B$ produces a product, such as luxury cars or travel, which is tax exempt for members of occupation $1A$. Under this arrangement, the aggregate elasticity of supply of market goods to the household sector exceeds the elasticity of demand primarily because the high wage group can switch to untaxed leisure and untaxed consumption of traded goods within the firm. The price of goods produced by the high wage occupation responds less to the tax than the price of goods produced by the low wage occupation. In this way the high wage group can shift a greater share of the burden of taxation to females in all households and to lower wage males. Consequently, the absolute burden of income taxation, as a selective trade tax, can be greater on lower income households.

If it were not possible for members of the high wage group to shift the tax to lower income households through this process, it could be argued that employment in its sector would eventually be reduced so as to achieve a similar incidence result. Switching to untaxed leisure or untaxed consumption of traded goods within the market sector can be seen as an immediate method for reducing the high wage group's labour supply to production for taxed trade in order to maintain the relative wage position of its members.

5.6   A reinterpretation of the rules for optimal taxation with leisure untaxable

The trade tax model of the incidence of income taxation employs the simplifying assumption that each individual produces in one sector only. There is no production for trade between individuals *within* the market sector nor *within* the household sector. Consequently, a tax on market goods traded with the household sector is effectively a tax on all traded goods in the economy and is analogous to a direct tax on all wage incomes. Leisure in both the market and household sectors is untaxed. Aggregate leisure in the market sector is given by the production of goods for own consumption, nx^1, and in the household sector by my^2. Labour supplied to work is strictly labour supplied to production for trade; the aggregate quantities of traded goods are mx^2 and ny^1 in the market and household sectors, respectively. An individual's wage income in sector 1 is $p\gamma x^2$, and in sector 2, y^1/γ. If the untaxability of leisure in both sectors imposes the only distortionary constraint on tax design, the rules derived by the standard optimal tax model can apply. The only points of departure from conventional theory lie in the specification of work and leisure used to interpret the rules and in second round effects introduced by circular production. However, if household structure results from binding institutional constraints the theory requires more serious modification.

Additional constraints may also be imposed by restrictions on job choices. The conclusion drawn in the previous sections, that income taxation can be regressive, depends on the premise that institutional restrictions on employment prevent taxed traded goods and leisure from being close substitutes for low wage earners when they are close substitutes for high wage earners. Because of the effect of these controls on the elasticity of substitution between traded goods and leisure, the tax base, wage income, can decline as the net wage rate increases. In optimal tax theory this condition is precluded by (4.2) which requires that the change in wage income in response to a change in the net wage rate be positive or zero. When this condition does not hold a progressive tax cannot redistribute income. But the condition may generally fail to hold when institutional restrictions allow crowding groups to switch to untaxed consumption in the market sector in response to taxes on trade between the sectors. In the tax literature this possibility is considered anomalous and has been ignored.

Optimal commodity taxation depends on the degree of substitution between taxed traded goods and leisure and the optimal tax parameters for a direct tax depend on the compensated substitution effect of taxed work and untaxed leisure. Since we are considering the special case of a composite market commodity which is traded for a composite household commodity, institutional restrictions controlling substitution effects have the same implications for both direct and indirect optimal tax models. Consider the Sheshinski (1972) result for an optimal linear income tax in an economy of individuals with identical utility functions and a distribution of wages, $f(w)$, determined by innate abilities. From the first order conditions we have

$$\int_0^\infty \left\{ (-u_1 + \lambda)\, w\hat{l} + \lambda \beta w \frac{\partial \hat{l}}{\partial \beta} \right\} f(w)\, dw = 0 \qquad (5.8)$$

where u_1 is the marginal utility of consumption expenditure which is interpreted here as a composite commodity obtained from trade; $\hat{l}$ is the optimal labour supply, λ is the social marginal utility of tax revenue and β is the marginal tax rate.

From the Slutsky result

$$\frac{\partial l}{\partial \beta} = -ws - w\hat{l}\, \frac{\partial \hat{l}}{\partial \alpha}$$

The substitution effect, s, the compensated labour supply response to a change in the net wage, is given by

$$s = \left(\frac{\partial \hat{l}}{\partial (1 - \beta)}\, w \right)_{\bar{u}} \geqq 0 \qquad (5.9)$$

Using (5.9), (5.8) can be written as

$$\int_0^\infty \left(\frac{-u_1}{\lambda} - \beta w \frac{\partial \hat{l}}{\partial \alpha} + 1 - \frac{\beta ws}{\hat{l}} \right) w\hat{l} f(w)\, dw = 0 \qquad (5.10)$$

The net social marginal valuation of income is given by

$$b = \frac{u_1}{\lambda} + \beta w \frac{\partial \hat{l}}{\partial \alpha}$$

Substituting into (5.10) gives

$$\int_0^\infty \left(1 - b + \frac{\beta ws}{\hat{l}} \right) w\hat{l} f(w)\, dw = 0$$

This result indicates that the tax rate depends upon the compensated labour supply elasticity and the way in which the marginal social valuation of incomes varies with the wage.

In the presence of a linear tax on all wage incomes, and with the definition of work as production for trade and of leisure as production for own consumption, we can write the substitution effects for representative individuals from sector 1 and sector 2, respectively, as

$$s^1 = \left(\frac{\partial x^2}{\partial(1-\beta)w^1}\right)_{\bar{u}}$$

$$s^2 = \left(\frac{\partial y^1}{\partial(1-\beta)w^2}\right)_{\bar{u}}$$

Although individuals have identical utility functions, when labour is restricted to employment in the household sector, we have

$$s^1 > s^2$$

The optimal linear tax rate is higher the lower the elasticity of the aggregate labour supply. However, in the presence of institutional restrictions, this elasticity is reduced precisely because the labour supply elasticity of the low wage group is reduced by the restrictions. If the institutional restrictions are not identified the tax is likely to be above the optimal rate. The low income groups may contribute the greater amount of revenue intended to redistribute income.

By ignoring institutional restrictions, different labour supply responses and levels of wage income can be attributed to relative preferences for leisure. Individuals employed in different occupations can be assumed to have equal full incomes before-tax. Although a greater burden of tax falls on individuals employed in the sector with the low elasticity of substitution between traded goods and leisure, conventional theory would tell us that the tax is essentially on individuals with a preference for working in the kind of job offered by sector 2.

The specification of work and leisure alters the interpretation of labour supply functions estimated from data for total time supplied to market activity. Estimates of market sector labour supply responses conventionally used for determining the distortionary impact of income taxation are inadequate because they do not distinguish the supply of labour to market production for trade from market sector leisure. At the same time, labour supply to production for trade in the household sector is ignored. Such estimates, therefore, aggregate labour supply and leisure in both the market and household sectors, identifying the former as labour supply to work and the latter as leisure.

There are further implications for the theory of optimal indirect taxation. The optimal indirect tax model with leisure untaxable derives the general rule that there should be higher taxes on those goods which are more complementary with leisure.[5] In a multi-commodity model, leisure is represented as a single additional commodity rather than as the production of commodities for own consumption. It is not appropriate to treat leisure as an additional commodity since both leisure and traded goods can consist of the same goods. The rule that complements to leisure be taxed more highly means that traded goods which are complements to goods produced for own consumption be taxed more highly. If it is assumed that trade occurs only between the market and household sectors, the rule can be interpreted more generally to require that goods traded between the two sectors be taxed more highly if market goods are complements to household leisure or if household services are complements to market leisure. In the absence of institutional restrictions, there is no apriori reason to expect traded goods and leisure to be more complementary in either sector. But if institutional restrictions make traded goods and leisure more complementary in the household sector, we have

$$s_{yx}^1 > s_{xy}^2$$

where

s_{yx}^1 is the substitution effect between traded household goods, y^1, and market goods for own consumption, x^1, for individuals in sector 1: and,

s_{xy}^2 is the substitution effect between traded market goods, x^2, and household goods for own consumption, y^2, for individuals in sector 2.

If higher rates of tax are imposed on commodities with lower demand elasticities as required for efficiency, this means that the burden of the tax can be absolutely greater on low wage individuals. Institutional restrictions can thus induce patterns of demand which are consistent with traded goods, which would be taxed more highly for efficiency reasons, being inferior with respect to full income. This implies that the tax base (traded goods) may decline with the wage.

It is important to recognise that the tax is on the quantity of good traded and not on the good per se. The traded quantity of a taxed good may decline with income yet the total quantity of the good obtained may not decline. High wage individuals may avoid the tax by switching to the consumption of the good within their own sector. Such methods of tax avoidance are frequently concealed by empirical estimates of demand elasticities which consider only the traded component of market sector outputs. Moreover, empirical estimates of demand elasticities for market goods by household conceal differences in the demand elasticities of individuals within households. Consequently the distribution of tax burdens within the household is not identified. This has implications not only for inequality within the household and for tax shifting between households as identified in section 5.5 but, in addition, it may increase the distortionary effect of commodity taxation.

5.7 Optimal taxation with leisure and wage income within the market sector and within the household untaxable

Ideally, we require a formulation of the optimal tax problem which specifies constraints causing institutional inequality and which takes account of second round effects introduced by circular production. In addition, it is necessary to specify sources of wage income which are likely to remain untaxed for institutional reasons. In Jones and Savage (forthcoming) optimal tax rules are derived subject to the constraint that wage income from intra-sector trade is untaxable. The results thus have implications for the optimal tax structure when wage income from production for trade within the firm and between firms within the market sector is untaxed and, in the household sector, wage income from production for trade between couples who share household chores is untaxed. The analysis does not introduce institutional inequality. The models employ a household welfare function in which individual labour supply is disaggregated into labour supplies earning taxed and untaxed wage incomes. In the formulation of the indirect tax problem, untaxed traded goods are distinguished from taxed traded goods.

The results obtained by Jones and Savage provide insights into a number of issues. The first order conditions can be interpreted in terms of the trade-off between efficiency and equity in tax design when opportunities for leisure in the firm and for receiving untaxed sources of wage income (or untaxed traded goods) increase with the market sector wage. This is the issue discussed in section 5.5. There is no longer a trade-off when the tax becomes regressive in terms of absolute burdens because of institutional restrictions on the employment of low wage males and of females.

A second issue which the analysis clarifies relates to the taxation of single earner and two earner couples. The optimal tax models in Apps and Jones (1980) take account of the untaxability of the wage income of dependent spouses and identify the trade-off between the equity gains from higher taxation of the market sector income of the single earner couple (higher taxation having the effect of taxing indirectly the untaxed wage income of dependent spouses) and the efficiency loss due to the distortionary effects of taxation. An objection to higher taxation of single earner households may be made on the grounds that the analysis does not take account of a division of labour and production for non-monetised trade within the two earner household. An extreme assumption is that in the single earner household only the dependent spouse produces household services, whereas in two earner households there is extensive 'sharing' of household chores. Thus, individuals in two earner households avoid tax on wage income (although a non-monetised source of wage income) just as the dependent spouse does. However, to the extent that individuals forming two earner couples are employed in lower wage market jobs, a modification to the tax structure to tax indirectly this source of wage income would introduce an element of regressivity. Moreover, the objection ignores leisure and untaxed sources of wage income within the market sector which can make the overall tax system absolutely regressive on true individual incomes and on true joint incomes.

5.8   A note on the interpretation of labour supply responses

Empirical studies indicate that the labour supply function for males in their prime working years is backward bending[6] or vertical[7], whereas for females it is forward rising. Boskin (1973) and Hall (1973) report a money wage elasticity for wives which is positive and greater than that of husbands. Boskin (1973) summarises the market sector employment differences between men and women as follows:

As important as the few cases of strong positive substitution effects is the complete lack of evidence of positive substitution effects for the most important group in the labour force – husbands. Husbands are the most important group for two reasons: they work the most, have the highest wages and, therefore, earn the most income of any group [p. 178].

When institutional restrictions are ignored, different male and female labour supply functions are attributed to different preferences for household activity and market work. To avoid the premise that women have a preference for leisure, Mincer (1962) and Gronau (1977) distinguish home work and home leisure and suggest that women have a preference for home work whereas men have a preference for market work.

With institutional constraints it is not necessary to attribute different labour supply responses to differences in preferences. If sector 1 represents high wage market jobs and sector 2 low wage market jobs and the household sector, individuals in sector 2 cannot enter sector 1 but can move between low wage market jobs and household activity. Prime age males are employed predominantly in sector 1, and they do not alter time allocated to the market sector in response to a fall in the net market wage because their jobs still offer higher after-tax full incomes than household activity. Women are mostly in sector 2 and, in response to a fall in the net market wage, they switch from market to household employment to equate net wages in these two sub-markets of sector 2. Thus, when there are institutional constraints on job choices, it cannot be inferred that labour supply functions for males and females differ because of differences in tastes. Moreover, conventional labour supply studies which estimate functions with time allocated to the market sector as the dependent variable, do not estimate labour supply functions. In response to a fall in the net market wage, prime age males may switch to leisure in the market sector while women switch to household production for trade as dependent spouses. The total labour supply of females may actually increase: it is only males who switch to leisure. This pattern of labour supply responses, which is encouraged by joint taxation,[8] reinforces regressivity in the incidence of income taxation.

An explanation for a backward bending supply curve is that

individuals in sector 1 can impose further restrictions on entry to maintain their relative wage positions. Such action involves an institutional change in the sector employment ratio. We now consider a model which introduces this kind of response to progressive income taxation.

6

The incidence of progressive income taxation under institutional inequality

6.1 A progressive income tax under crowding inequality

It is evident that most forms of direct taxation and indirect taxes are taxes on trade between the market and household sectors. The analysis of the preceding chapter has shown that under the kinds of institutional restrictions which characterise modern economies, it is possible for a greater share of the absolute burden of this trade taxation to be shifted to low wage groups in crowded activities. A greater absolute burden can fall on low wage labour in the crowded household sector and, when higher wage market occupation groups have greater opportunities for leisure in the firm, a greater absolute burden of income taxation can fall on lower income households. Income taxation may therefore increase inequality and simultaneously increase the excess burden of crowding.

In response to this result it might be argued that the problem lies in the definition of the tax base; if the tax base could be broadened to include production for own consumption in the market and household sectors, or if the wage rate could be taxed, a progressive tax would reduce inequality. In optimal tax theory the objection to a proposal of this kind is that labour supply is unobservable and therefore only an indicator of full income or of the wage can be taxed. This chapter identifies a second fundamental problem. Institutional restrictions imply additional constraints on tax design. The institutional organization of the economy may facilitate responses by high wage groups which shift the burden of taxation irrespective of whether the tax base is full income, or the Haig-Simons comprehensive definition of income interpreted to include the trade value of own consumption.

85

An important aspect of the organization of the economy under crowding is that inequality is sector related. Differences in wages or in full incomes between individuals correspond to differences between sectors. An income tax regime which imposes larger amounts of tax on higher wage individuals is thus a selective employment tax. The effect of the tax depends on the extent to which those sectors can control the economy. In contrast, when inequality in wages is due to innate ability differences, the distribution of ability can be expected to be identical for each occupation, provided the population is sufficiently large. Unless non-uniform differences in innate abilities or tastes cause employment segregation, wage inequality between individuals will not correspond to wage differences between sectors.[1] Hence a tax system imposing larger amounts of tax on higher income individuals is not a selective employment tax. It is equivalent to a proportional tax on the aggregate full income of each sector.

The following section examines the incidence of income taxation as a tax on a high wage sector under alternative assumptions about the high wage group's response to tax in terms of further controls on employment. In the cases considered, the income tax is partly shifted and may, under certain conditions, add to the distortionary effects of crowding while achieving little or no improvement in equality. Section 6.3 comments on some implications of treating a high wage occupation group as a cartel. The final section of the chapter briefly notes the incidence of benefits from public projects which are financed by central government from tax revenue and which provide 'local' public goods for sectors which are 'local' communities.

6.2.   The incidence of income taxation

Under certain conditions, a tax on the income from a factor in fixed supply such as innate ability cannot be shifted. The tax is also non-distortionary. Mieszkowski (1969) discusses this result in the context of the following simplifying assumptions adopted in general equilibrium analyses of tax incidence:

   (i) perfectly competitive commodity and factor markets;
   (ii) a closed economy;

(iii) perfect factor mobility; and,

(iv) a perfectly inelastic supply of factors.

If individuals have uniformly different innate productivities, and this is the only source of inequality, it can be shown that the above result holds under these conditions provided the tax base is full income and individual preferences are homothetic. When ability is not sector specific, there is no change in before-tax wages. The effective incidence of the tax corresponds to its formal incidence. Thus, with inequality originating from innate ability differences in a competitive labour market with perfect labour mobility, a progressive tax with full income as the tax base can be fully effective in reducing inequality and it can be non-distortionary. But income is earned from the supply of acquired ability, as well as innate ability. Condition (iv) holds only with respect to innate ability.[2] The supply of acquired ability depends on an individual's previous wage, and if the first round effect of the tax is to reduce wages, this lowers the rate at which ability is acquired. Nevertheless, provided ability is not sector specific and preferences are homothetic, the effective incidence of the tax can still correspond to its formal incidence.

In contrast, with crowding, greater ability is sector specific and a progressive income tax is equivalent to a set of selective employment taxes. In this case, to determine the incidence of a progressive income tax, we consider the effects of a selective tax on the incomes of individuals in sector 1. Individuals are assumed to possess innately identical tastes and productivities. Group 1 receives a higher wage than group 2 because group 1 is employed in the crowding sector and group 2 in the crowded sector. When the tax is introduced, the income of individuals in group 1 depends on the price ratio p and the tax, t. The incidence of the tax is examined under two alternative assumptions about the ability of the high wage group to change its entry quota in response to the tax. The assumptions can be interpreted as:

(i) a period of time during which the sector employment ratio is fixed (there is not sufficient time to change numbers in response to the tax by altering existing labour mobility restrictions); and,

(ii) a period of time during which the sector employment ratio is variable (the high wage group can further restrict entry in response to the tax).

As in the crowding model, the effects for cases (i) and (ii) are defined for the short and the long run.

(i) Fixed sector employment ratio:
When the sector employment ratio cannot be altered, the equilibrium condition is given by

$$x^1(p, \, px(p, \, t)) + \bar{y}x^2(p, \, y(p)) = x(p, \, t)$$

In the short run, since individual outputs are fixed at $\bar{x}$ and $\bar{y}$, the actual incidence is the same as the formal incidence: the tax burden is entirely on group 1. In subsequent production periods, individuals in sector 1 have a lower net-of-tax income for investment in capital. Hence they become relatively less productive. In the long run

$$\left[\frac{\partial p}{\partial t} \right]_L = \frac{\dfrac{\partial x}{\partial t}(1 - px_{px}^1)}{x_p^1 + xx_{px}^1 + \dfrac{\partial x}{\partial p}(p-1) + \gamma\left(x_p^2 + x_y^2 \dfrac{\partial y}{\partial p} \right)} > 0$$

for $y_y^2 < 1$, y_{px}^1, $\dfrac{\partial x}{\partial p} > 0$, $\dfrac{\partial y}{\partial p} < 0$, which are the conditions on (2.12), and

for $\dfrac{\partial x}{\partial t} < 0$.

Although the number of individuals employed in each sector is fixed, the tax on individual incomes in sector 1 is partly shifted because of second round effects on individual productivities. If second round effects are ignored, it might be inferred that the tax burden falls entirely on the high wage group because individual and aggregate allocations of time to sector 1 are unchanged. However, a high wage individual does not alter time allocated to sector 1 because after-tax full income remains higher than for alternative employment.

(ii) Variable sector employment ratio:
We now assume the sector employment ratio can be changed in response to the tax. The short run equilibrium condition is given by

$$x^1(p, \, p\bar{x}) + \gamma(t)x^2(p, \, \bar{y}) = \bar{x}$$

which, assuming a unique interior solution for p, yields

$$\left[\frac{\partial p}{\partial t} \right]_s = \frac{-\gamma_t x^2}{x_p^1 + xx_{p\bar{x}}^1 + \gamma x_p^2} > 0$$

for $y_{p\bar{x}}^1$, $\gamma_t > 0$. The long run equilibrium condition is given by

$$x^1(p, \, px(p, \, t)) + \gamma(t)x^2(p, \, y(p)) = x(p, \, t)$$

which yields

$$\left[\frac{\partial p}{\partial t}\right]_L = \frac{\dfrac{\partial x}{\partial t}(1 - px_{px}^1) - \gamma_t x^2}{x_p^1 + xx_{px}^1 + \dfrac{\partial x}{\partial p}(px_{px}^1 - 1) + \gamma\left(x_p^2 + x_y^2\dfrac{\partial y}{\partial p}\right)} > 0$$

for $y_y^2 < 1$, y_{px}^1, $\dfrac{\partial x}{\partial p}$, $\gamma_t > 0$, $\dfrac{\partial y}{\partial p}$, $\dfrac{\partial y}{\partial p}$, $\dfrac{\partial x}{\partial t} < 0$. As well as the usual conditions, the incidence of the tax depends upon γ_t; that is, upon the extent to which the taxed high wage group in sector 1 can further crowd sector 2.

Further crowding in response to income taxation may involve an increase in the number of individuals classified as unemployed. In this case it is not the work disincentive effect of increased taxation on market sector incomes which reduces employment in the market sector. What is identified as a disincentive effect reflects the decision by high wage groups to maintain their relative wage position by further restricting entry. The analysis can be generalised for a multi-sector economy with a hierarchical structure of wages.

It is interesting to compare implications of these models with the general equilibrium analysis of the excess burden of differential taxes on market labour and capital in Boskin (1975). Boskin hypothesises that there is a reallocation of the capital stock and labour force between market and household sectors because capital and labour are taxed more heavily in the market than in the home. In contrast to Harberger (1962), Boskin recognises the use of labour and capital in household production but otherwise employs the standard assumptions of tax incidence analysis: factors are perfectly mobile between sectors and factors are in fixed supply. Factors are not produced and there is no production for consumption in the market sector or for trade in the household sector.

Boskin calculates that factors are taxed at the following rates expressed as percentages of gross factor incomes

Market capital 61%

$$
\begin{array}{ll}
\text{Market labour} & 29\% \\
\text{Household capital} & 18\% \\
\text{Household labour} & 0\% \\
\end{array}
$$

Using the Harberger (1962) model and estimates of elasticities, the welfare cost of the preferential tax treatment of household activity is calculated to be approximately 20 to 40 billion dollars (or seven to thirteen percent of tax revenues).

Hours of work in the household sector are calculated as the difference between 2,000 hours and the amount of time working in the market sector. The calculation implies that the total labour supply to work for each individual is fixed at 8 hours a day for five days of a 50 week year.[3] The time spent working in the home is valued at the after-tax wage on the grounds that: 'This provides a lower bound on the value of the marginal unit of work in the home, since we may infer from an individual's full-time work in the home that the valuation of time in the house, at the margin, is no less than in the market' (p. 7). However, when the aggregate and individual labour time allocated to market sector occupations is subject to institutional constraints, the after-tax market wage does not provide a lower bound for the value of time used in household production. Differential rates of tax will only encourage individuals in crowded market sector jobs to transfer to a crowded household sector. They will not encourage prime age males to transfer, unless the higher taxes on market sector employment more than offset differences in wage rates caused by institutional restrictions.[4] A larger distortion is likely to be associated with institutional restrictions. A similar argument applies in respect of higher taxes on market sector capital.

The Boskin paper also presents the following estimates for units (billions) of capital and labour services in the market and in the home:

$$
\begin{array}{ll}
\text{Market capital} & 798 \\
\text{Market labour} & 154 \\
\text{Household capital} & 240 \\
\text{Household labour} & 150 \\
\end{array}
$$

The figures indicate that market output is relatively labour intensive. However, a comparison of capital and labour ratios using these figures may be misleading. Market labour includes the total allocation of time to market activity, and this includes the allocation of time to own consumption in the market sector. In contrast, household labour excludes 16 hours a day (and weekends) from the total allocation of time to the household sector by each individual. Total physical capital in both sectors is included. For consistency, either the component of household capital[5] which is an input to leisure should be subtracted to derive comparable capital labour ratios or the figure for household labour should include all individual time in the household sector. Human capital in both sectors is omitted from capital and included in labour and this would also lead to an underestimate of the capital intensity of the market sector. Casual observation suggests that it is the market sector which is relatively capital intensive with regard to both physical and human capital, a phenomenon which is explained by crowding.

In many instances the taxes listed by Boskin are not levied on total factor payments but on payments for the supply of factors to market production for 'trade' between the market and household sectors. The results of the previous chapter apply where the taxes induce a reallocation of resources from production for 'trade' to production for own consumption in the firm, especially in the high wage jobs.

6.3 Income taxation and occupation cartels

The model of crowding in Chapter 2 introduces inequality by an exogenous change in the sector employment ratio, and the preceding analysis of taxation assumes an exogenous but variable employment ratio. The underlying argument is that unless the introduction of a progressive tax changes the distribution of power, there is no justification for assuming that the tax reduces inequality. Institutional inequality reflects the distribution of power and if the tax leaves the power structure unchanged, we can expect institutions to reorganize employment and production in a way which enables the burden of tax to be shifted. The reorganization of the economy imposes an additional efficiency cost without reducing inequality. The aim of the two sector model with a variable sector employment ratio is to capture this kind of political response to taxation.

A possible objection to the model is the representation of power by a sector employment ratio which is exogenous to the model. It may be suggested that the sector employment ratio should be treated as an endogenous variable. However, as noted in Chapter 2, a model such as a revenue maximizing cartel model, which treats employment as an endogenous variable, does not indicate the way in which the power structure has developed. The initial distribution of power is taken as given just as in the model above.

In the context of cartels, it is interesting to note a difficulty which arises in explaining the perpetuation of inequality. In particular, if a simple revenue maximising cartel model is used to represent high wage occupations which collude to set fees and entry quotas, a progressive tax can, in principle, undermine the power and income position of the cartel. If a high wage group behaves as a revenue maximising cartel, the group sets price and employment to maximize revenue given by

$$R = (p - T(p, t))x^d(p) \qquad T \leq p$$

where $x^d(p)$ is aggregate demand for the good at price p, t is the tax parameter and the tax on price, T, depends on price and the tax parameter.

From the first order condition we find that there can only be a stable equilibrium if the demand function is negatively sloped and we also find that the group continues to function as a revenue maximizing cartel only if

$$T/p = T_p$$

That is, if the average rate of tax is greater than the marginal rate, the cartel shifts a part of the tax burden by reducing employment. If the average and proportional rates of tax are equal, employment is unchanged and the tax burden falls entirely on individuals in the cartel. If the tax is progressive, it breaks down the cartel. When we observe that the power of high income groups who practice entry restrictions is not broken down by progressive income taxation, we can infer that a cartel model does not capture the mechanism whereby inequality is perpetuated. Alternatively, it might be argued that the income tax is not progressive because leisure and various sources of wage income are untaxed.

From a cartel model it is clear that, in the presence of institutional constraints, observed responses to taxation are not labour supply responses in the usual sense. A cartel model precludes the existence of a labour supply function and therefore an explanation of labour supply responses in terms of income and substitutional effects.

6.4 The incidence of benefits from public projects

The above analysis has shown possible effects of a progressive income tax as a tax on high wages, under the assumption that inequality is due to crowding. We now consider the incidence of benefits from public projects under a similar assumption. The assumption we choose is that public projects involve the production of goods which are 'public' to individuals within a local community but private to different communities, and the different communities are the crowding and crowded sectors of our model. In other words, the central government spends tax revenue on local public goods where the local communities are not formed purely as a response to scale economies. Instead, group formation is controlled institutionally and corresponds to occupations or sectors of the crowding model.

Let the level of output in each sector be a constant returns to scale function of services from public projects as well as labour. If r^1 and r^2 denote the per capita supplies of publicly produced services to sectors 1 and 2, respectively, sector production functions take the form

$$x = x(k^1, r^1)$$
$$y = y(k^2, r^2)$$

Let

$$r^1 + r^2 = 1$$
$$k^1 + k^2 = 1$$

so that

$$y = y(1 - k^1, 1 - r^1)$$

The government's objective is to maximize total utility given by

$$W = W(x(k^1, r^1), y(1 - k^1, 1 - r^1))$$

The first order conditions can be written as

$$\frac{W_x}{W_y} = \frac{y_{r^1} + y_{k^1}}{x_{r^1} + x_{k^1}} = p$$

or as

$$p(x_{r1} + x_{k1}) = y_{r1} + y_{k1}$$

If k^1 and k^2 are fixed

$$p = \frac{y_{r1}}{x_{r1}}$$

Thus, if p increases because of crowding, r increases, and conversely. We can conclude that the incidence of benefits from public projects financed from central government can exacerbate crowding inequality.

Such a situation would arise when central government projects are selected on cost benefit criteria calculated on the basis of existing market prices and imputed values. An example is the planning of transport networks and services. We could expect to observe a systematic bias towards the provision of services advantaging high wage sectors, without compensating contributions to tax revenue by beneficiaries.[6] It could be argued that this bias characterises the public provision of services for the market and household sectors for there appears to be a tendency for central government to choose projects which are of greater benefit to the market sector than to household activities.

7

Population growth and family policy

7.1 Child dependency and optimal population policy

The family in traditional societies is seen as the institutional response to reproduction and the support of children and of the aged. Parents choose to have children for old age security and for the 'joys of parenthood'. The nuclear family in modern societies is concerned primarily with reproduction and the nurturing of children since social security tax-transfer schemes have reduced the dependency of the aged on the family. From the point of view of intergenerational trade discussed in Chapter 3, this development enables intergenerational trade between stages B and C of the life cycle to occur largely outside the family. Although State funding of education and other services for children permits trade between stages A and B to take place to some extent outside the family, a large part of intergenerational trade between these two age groups remains restricted to the family. The question arises as to whether State social security or pension schemes for retirement, which are unaccompanied by a symmetrical program in respect of children, influence population growth.[1]

The accepted thesis, that social security for the aged to the extent that it undermines the old age security motivation for reproduction, can contribute to a reduced rate of population growth is based on the premise that there are no additional distortions. In section 7.2 it is contended that transfers to the aged are unlikely to offset institutional constraints on the employment of women, on household size and on the rearing of children. It is argued that these constraints encourage population growth and that joint taxation, by reinforcing these constraints, has the same effect. In view of the relationship between child

95

dependency upon the family and crowding inequality identified in Chapter 3, the introduction of substantial transfers to children, accompanied by measures to eliminate institutional constraints on the employment of women, is proposed as a direction for family and population policy designed to improve equality and per capita welfare. Section 7.3 focuses on the effects of joint taxation on the employment choices of women. Chapter 4 examined the distortionary and distributional effects of joint taxation under the assumption that job choices and wage income inequality among males reflect given endowments and tastes. Here the analysis introduces institutional inequality in market sector wages and in household wages for dependent spouses. The taxation of couples and of families on the basis of joint market sector money incomes is identified as a tax policy which reinforces institutional inequality between families and between men and women. Section 7.4 comments on technical considerations in the design of an optimal child support policy. A primary objective of the policy is to discourage the perpetuation of institutional inequality through the dependence of children upon parent income. The optimal scheme implies an optimal population policy and may have consequences for the stabilization of cyclical fluctuations in the rate of growth of the economy.

7.2 Population growth effects of restrictions on the employment of women

Let us suppose that the optimum rate of population growth is zero and that individuals are innately identical. They invest only in human capital and live 80 years with optimum lifetime consumption and production profiles as depicted in Figure 3.1. In the absence of institutional restrictions they make reproduction decisions and trade in an environment which permits a Pareto efficient intertemporal equilibrium. The limitation of intergenerational trade to the family implies that, in the economy of Figure 3.1, each individual during stage B of the life cycle repays debt incurred in childhood by supporting an aged person and saves for retirement by rearing a child; the debt incurred in childhood is exactly equal to saving for old age. In this economy the introduction of a social security tax-transfer scheme for retirement breaks the link between reproduction and old age security. If old age security were the only motivation for reproduction, population would fall to zero. To the extent that the enjoyment of children to parents[2] is also a consideration, the population level is less affected but nevertheless its rate of growth declines. If there are additional conditions encouraging population growth, this simple result may no longer hold.

When women are restricted by social attitudes and the tax structure to the household sector, and to a production unit which is limited in size so that they cannot produce all goods as efficiently as individuals employed in firms, they specialize in the production of goods which are least associated with scale economies. If the same scale economies can be achieved in the production of all goods, labour constrained to the household may obtain relatively improved terms of trade by producing those goods which firms are not permitted to produce. In particular, when children are not produced in firms,[3] female labour constrained to the household sector may receive a higher wage by specializing in household child rearing. By this means, the household sector may produce a product for which there is no perfect substitute in the market sector. Indeed, unless such an opportunity exists, not only does the wage differential between the two sectors reflect the full effect of the efficiency loss due to constraints on household size, but the burden of increments in income taxation as a tax on trade between the market and household sectors falls predominantly on women in the household sector. The burden of the tax can be shifted only by producing a product for trade for which there is no perfect substitute in the market sector, such as own children for men. In this way institutional constraints on the employment of women and on child rearing can encourage population growth, and joint taxation can reinforce the population growth effect. We have an explanation for the biological growth rate in terms of opportunity wage rates for women: on account of social attitudes and tax policy, women may be better off producing children even though the wage for that activity is low.

Whether transfers to the aged reduce population growth below an optimal level depends on whether the transfers reverse the effect on population of institutional constraints and taxation on the employment of women. Assuming that there exists an optimum intermediate rate of population growth,[4] transfers to children financed from a tax on prime aged adults may be commended as a solution to the distortionary population growth effect of a social security tax and transfer scheme for the aged. However, such a comprehensive age tax-transfer scheme is a first best policy. Unless the scheme is accompanied by measures to abolish distortionary constraints imposed by social attitudes towards the employment of women and by a change to true individual taxation, the scheme cannot be expected to achieve an optimum population policy.

An increase in government transfers to children and the abolition of restrictions on the employment of women can be justified not only from the viewpoint of population policy but in terms of social justice. There would be increased equality between men and women. As discussed in Chapter 3, the dependence of children upon parents among whom there is institutional crowding provides a crucial mechanism for perpetuating institutional inequality from one generation to the next within families. An age related tax-transfer scheme based on the principle of raising revenue for transfers to children and the aged by a tax on prime age adults could provide children with access to their potentially more equal lifetime incomes. If children emerge from stage A more noticeably equal, institutional inequality may become more difficult to maintain.

In addition, if institutional restrictions provide high income groups with wider choices in consumption and better opportunities for investing savings for retirement than low income groups, high income groups can be less dependent upon children for current consumption and for retirement. We might thus expect higher income groups to have fewer children. Institutional restrictions causing crowding may explain, in part, variation in reproduction decisions by income. If low income families tend to have more children, the failure to introduce substantial transfers to children, in cash or in kind, leaves the major burden of child support on low income parents. This has implications for crowding in subsequent generations: crowding inequality may increase due to variation in population growth rates by income.

There are also consequences for equality within the family. Distortionary constraints on the employment of women encourage inequality by sex and thus between spouses within the family. Apps and Stiglitz (1979) assume parents invest optimally in their children.[5]

Knowning that the average female wage is less than the male wage and that children must pair from different households, parents' optimal investment leads to systematic discrimination against their daughters. Inequality by sex is perpetuated within the family. The models show how income taxation as a tax on trade between market and household sectors exacerbates the well recognised phenomenon of parents' investing less in their daughters.

One might also develop a theory linking the structure of female wage rates and population changes to short term cyclical trends. It is frequently observed that the market sector labour force participation rate of women increases with upswings in the market sector of the economy. As the relative price of market goods rises, the relative market sector wage rises and so women switch to market sector employment until net-of-tax wage rates equalize. As a result, market sector output increases and the wage falls. At the same time, the rate of population growth declines because of the fall in labour supply to the household sector. The resulting shift in demand exacerbates the fall in the price of market goods. As the market sector wage rate falls because of these supply and demand effects, the likely political response by the more powerful groups in the market sector is the introduction of measures to force women back into the household sector in order to maintain previous wage differentials. We would expect to see an emphasis on social values concerning the 'proper' employment of women and attempts to extend joint taxation of couples by introducing further tax concessions or transfers for females dependent upon market sector earners.

If such measures achieve their objective, the labour force participation rate of women declines with downturns in the market sector of the economy. As women return to the household sector the birth rate rises. This, in turn, can contribute to the initiation of the next upswing in the economy, together with the price effect of a fall in the supply of market goods as women leave the market sector. In the long run, there may be a positive rate of population growth, although the actual growth rate in the short run may fluctuate cyclically in this way. The cycle would, of course, be interrupted and the long run rate of population growth altered were it to prove impossible to convince the younger generation of women to be employed full time in the low wage household sector.

7.3   Joint taxation and institutional inequality

The analyses of Chapter 4 and of the preceding section suggest that the taxation of couples on a joint income basis cannot be justified on either efficiency or equity grounds. This section examines joint taxation in the context of institutional inequality among households. It is assumed that households are formed by pairs of adults of opposite sex and that market sector workers are constrained to purchasing household services from a dependent spouse. The tax system allows tax avoidance by the dependency of one spouse upon a market sector earner within each pair of adults forming a household. For simplicity, men are assumed to be employed only in the market sector and, as in Chapter 5 (section 5.5), in one of two occupation classes: a high wage crowding occupation or a low wage crowded occupation. Women are employed either in the household sector or in the crowded market occupation. As indicated in section 5.5, under these conditions crowding inequality between males in the market sector is reproduced among females employed as dependent spouses in the household sector. Women who marry high wage males are paid a higher wage in the household sector than women who marry low wage males. The explanation is that each man can marry only one wife and is thus constrained to trading market goods for household services produced by one individual. If the household wage for women married to high wage males is higher than the wage in the crowded market sector occupation, these women do not enter the market sector. However, women married to low wage males receive a correspondingly lower wage for household production for trade. They are therefore likely to supply labour to crowded market jobs.

The wife of a low wage worker can thus be expected to supply labour to both the market sector for a wage income which is taxed and to the household sector for a wage income which is untaxed.[6] Wage incomes from both are used to purchase market goods as factors of household production. Joint taxation under these conditions can be seen as an additional tax on the labour supply of the second market earner of low wage families. If second earners are female, joint taxation is a selective tax on the wage income of women employed in crowded market sector occupations and married to men also employed in crowded occupations. Two earner couples may have lower true money resources than single earner couples but, in order to justify joint taxation, this can be concealed by omitting the money wage income of the dependent spouse in the calculation of money resources. To the extent that joint taxation reduces the market sector wage incomes of women, it reduces their purchases of market goods for household production which, in turn, reduces their productivity in the household sector. As their household sector output falls, the price of household services for trade to low wage males rises. Consequently, the burden of the tax falls on both men and women in lower wage families. Joint taxation and other forms of discrimination against the market sector employment of women not only increase inequality between males and females but reinforce income differences between families.

This institutional theory for the determination of the wage incomes of dependent spouses can be contrasted with conventional theory which is based on the premise of 'sharing' between spouses. In conventional labour supply theory, an increase in husband income has an income and a substitution effect and, in addition, is associated with cross-income and cross-substitution effects on the wife's labour supply. The wife can be expected to spend less time at work, firstly because the increase in household income results in an increase in the household's consumption of leisure, and secondly because the husband tends to substitute his better paid labour time for that of his wife's. From this analysis it is concluded that the labour supply decision of any one family member depends on the wage rates available to all other household members. The analysis ignores the labour supply of the wife to household production for a money wage income. With an increase in the husband's wage, institutional constraints and tax avoidance by dependency explain an increase in the wife's wage for household production for trade and any consequent reduction in labour supply to market production for trade.

If the market sector labour force participation rate of women were to increase because of the abolition of all forms of joint taxation or because of a change in attitudes to the market sector employment of women, we might expect efforts to reinforce restrictions on the market sector employment of women not only on the part of crowding males but also by women married to high wage males. Due to life cycle variation in male incomes we might expect those women who oppose policies which increase the market sector participation of women to be relatively older. Women in such families, who remain out of the market sector because they married higher wage husbands, are at a stage of life when they are less able to compete for market jobs against younger women married to husbands also earning higher market wages. Indeed, a younger married pair may both work in lower wage market occupations and together obtain higher market sector money incomes than the single high wage earner of an older family. As a result, the *market* sector wage income differential between high and low occupation classes is observed to be reduced on a family basis. It may thus be in the interests of the older generation of high wage families and, in particular, the older generation of women in these families, that restrictions on the mobility of labour which existed when they were young continue to operate throughout their lifetime. It cannot always be assumed that those who support policies which exacerbate inequality on the basis of sex are necessarily concerned to achieve that outcome per se. The aim may be to discourage the market sector employment of females to sustain family inequality.

7.4 Family policy

In modern economies where social security provides for retirement and where there is extensive institutional inequality, consideration needs to be given to the introduction of a child support program which extends beyond public education and minimal cash payments. Cash transfers or in-kind benefits to children are likely to have opposite effects to taxation on a joint income basis. The latter can be characterised as a policy which exacerbates inequality among families and between men and women. In the presence of institutional inequality, increased benefits to children may reduce inequality between families and between individuals. Yet joint tax schemes and transfer payments to children are often presented as close alternatives. Many countries support progressive income tax systems on a joint income basis and provide relatively small payments or in-kind benefits for young children.

If inequality reflects given characteristics, the design of cash transfers to children is a conventional optimal tax problem which, as

Mirrlees (1972) explains, involves the usual adverse disincentive effects on labour supply and, as well, adverse incentive effects on population growth.[7] The co-ordination of benefits to children with social security provisions for the aged involves the design of a comprehensive age related tax-transfer scheme which can, in principle, offset the population growth incentive effects of transfers to children against the disincentive effects of transfers to the aged. A comprehensive age tax-transfer scheme is defined as an institutional arrangement which takes intergenerational trade outside the family over the entire life cycle. In stage B individuals are taxed and the revenue used to support children in stage A and the aged in stage C.

If social security for the aged is introduced without symmetrical treatment of children, having no children allows avoidance of the repayment of debt incurred in childhood. Those who have large families incur a disproportionate share of the social burden of child support. This can be an important distributional consideration if large families tend to have lower incomes. Aside from distortions arising from differences in the demand for child quantity, there is no intrinsic merit in an age tax-transfer scheme. If inequality is due entirely to given endowments and tastes, a progressive tax on the basis of adult incomes could be effective in redistributing incomes between parents and between children from different families, because a change in parents' incomes affects not only their work-leisure choices but, as well, their child quality and quantity decisions. However, in the presence of institutional inequality, we do not have the conventional efficiency-equity trade-off. Instead, there can be a gain in both efficiency and equity depending on the extent to which an age tax-transfer scheme can induce a decline in institutional inequality by providing children from different families access to their potentially more equal lifetime incomes.

The design of child support may be treated in a manner analogous to the optimal taxation of housing considered in Atkinson (1977b). Transfers in money or in kind reduce the price of children to parents,[8] and, as Becker and Lewis (1973) point out, a fall in the price of children can be partly shifted to parents by a reduction in their contribution to each child. If the transfers are large enough they may influence family size. If transfers to children are partly shifted to parents by a reduction in their contribution to each child, the transfers increase equality among children and among parents. This is obviously a desirable outcome. But in the presence of institutional inequality, intra-family shifting of taxes and transfers raise a fundamental dilemma. If crowding sectors can shift income taxation by increasing restrictions on entry into high wage market jobs, transfers to children to the extent that they are shifted to parents may ultimately become ineffective in reducing inter-family inequality. Within-family inequality may also be unchanged if the more powerful individuals within the family acquire a greater share of transfer payments. If transfers to children are to be effective, it may thus be necessary to introduce measures which prevent intra-family shifting of taxes and transfers. In other words, it may be necessary to design cash or in-kind transfers so as to guarantee that children are the primary beneficiaries.

There are two possible approaches to the problem. One is the provision of in-kind benefits which are independent of parents' contributions and increase the child's human capital. For example, State education may to some extent be independent of parents' inputs, such as food and clothing, and may contribute to the development of more equal abilities among children. The importance of the latter is to make institutional restrictions on entry in to high wage jobs more observable and hence increase the likelihood of opposition to the restrictions. Indeed, one might postulate that the long term historical trend towards equality in developed economies is explained by the State's increased contribution to education, and not by progressive income taxation. If State education is not offset by a fall in living standards at home due to reduced parent contributions, it may be relatively effective in enabling children to develop more similar abilities. If this thesis is correct, it provides a strong argument for in-kind services, such as day-care, health and education services for children. A second approach is through more direct regulatory control. To ensure that children are the beneficiaries of cash or in-kind transfers made to them, it may be necessary to introduce more stringent and more effective regulation of the living standards for children at home. The regulations would determine parents' minimum contribution per child and therefore prevent the reduction of parent contributions below a minimum standard.

The optimal tax problem to be resolved in the design of a child support scheme is the size of the transfer for each age. Transfers to cover the actual cost of full day-care in the market sector net of any current government contributions, are proposed in Apps (1975).[9] Although a policy of this kind is designed to reduce crowding inequality by improving the capital market for children and to meet the criteria of an optimal population policy, it may also contribute to stabilization policy. Such a policy for investment in the next generation may help to stabilize fluctuations in population growth caused by changing social attitudes towards the market sector employment of women.

8

Conclusions and directions for policy

8.1 Unemployment, factor intensities and tax incidence

The theory of crowding inequality presents a way in which institutional restrictions on the mobility of individuals distinguished by arbitrary characteristics can create inequality. A crucial feature of the theory is that society consists of individuals who each have a fixed endowment of time in every period. With circular production, unequal individual ownership of capital requires additional constraints. The theory indicates how institutional restrictions on entry into groups and occupations can produce capital ownership inequality and implies that the fundamental 'class' divisions are between individuals who, for historical reasons, have different power to influence institutions and thereby distort group formation, the composition of output, relative prices and factor intensities, to attain higher incomes. The models offer an explanation for the tendency of low wage labour to be employed in time intensive activity and high wage labour in capital intensive activity. The explanation departs from the usual approach to technological differences.

Much of the analysis focuses on the incidence of progressive income taxation under crowding inequality between market sector jobs and between the market and household sectors. A distinction is made between the technical meaning of work and leisure and the institutional interpretations of these activity categories. Labour supply is defined as the allocation of time to production for trade, and leisure as the allocation of time to production for own consumption. On the basis of these definitions, income taxation in modern economies is identified as selective trade taxation. In contrast to the standard optimal tax model based on the premise that all forms of wage incomes are taxable, the

107

analysis takes account of untaxed sources of wage incomes in the market and household sectors.

The study of income taxation as a tax on trade between the market and household sectors assumes that only wage income from labour supply to production for trade between the two sectors is taxed. Institutional restrictions on entry into market sector jobs and on the organization of household production are identified as causes of wage differences between the two sectors. Household production is the low wage and the time intensive sector. High wage market production is capital intensive. It is argued that the restrictions introduce not only inequality in incomes between the two sectors but also differences in elasticities of factor substitution by reducing the substitutability of factors in household production. With low substitutability between factors in household production, the demand for market goods by household producers is relatively inelastic. High substitutability of factors in market production allows the supply of market goods to the household sector to be relatively elastic. As a result, the burden of income taxation as a tax on trade between the market and household sectors can be greater on the low wage household sector. In addition, when opportunities for consumption in the market sector increase with the market wage, supply elasticities can be expected to increase with the market sector wage. Consequently, because of institutional constraints controlling income differences and supply and demand elasticities, the burden of income taxation can be greater on low income families.

The possibility of reversing these results by broadening the tax base is rejected on the grounds that such an outcome would require a decline in the power of high wage groups to influence institutions. A progressive tax on individual full incomes is, under institutional crowding, a selective occupation tax. More realistically, it might be assumed that the more powerful individuals would, in response to an increment in tax on their incomes, impose tighter restrictions on entry into their occupations so as to maintain their income positions. With variable quotas, a progressive tax with full income as the tax base can be shifted by reducing numbers in the crowding sectors of the economy. Income taxation is thus likely to increase numbers in low wage market occupations and, as well, in the household sector. The latter might be achieved in several ways. The number of individuals classified as unemployed might rise. Alternatively, the employment of women in the market sector might be further discouraged. Yet another method would be a reduction in the retirement age. Whatever the means, employment in the market sector falls.

These results suggest that theories which attribute unemployment to capital intensification or to the replacement of labour by capital in market sectors are open to question. Because the introduction of more capital intensive production processes and labour redundancy are observed simultaneously in market sectors, it is sometimes inferred that they are causally linked: that technological development causes unemployment. In contrast, if there are institutional restrictions, it is the resulting underemployment in the market sector which causes the sector to become relatively capital intensive. Higher wage occupations become capital intensive because their members have more income to invest. Middle wage activity comprising market sector jobs in which wages are controlled but not the entry of 'foreign' capital is likely to become capital intensive because of investment by both the higher and middle wage groups. In the long run, foreign investment increases crowding inequality and there is a reverse effect on factor intensities. Thus, irrespective of the source of investment, differences in capital intensity are related to crowding by high income occupations. Income taxation, to the extent that it exacerbates the tendency to increase crowding can encourage the capital intensification of market production. The relationship between the apparent 'need' for redistributional tax-subsidy schemes and the effects of such schemes can be self-reinforcing.

8.2 Policy implications of a crowding theory of inequality and tax incidence

The tax incidence analyses show that income tax-subsidy schemes can be ineffective in reducing inequality and can increase the distortionary effects of crowding. If inequality is to a large extent due to politically induced crowding, more effective measures may be those directed toward breaking down barriers to entry, such as the introduction of legislation to prohibit restrictions on factor mobilities. In many instances existing legislation protects such restrictions. Clearly, the feasibility of new legislation of this kind is a political issue. It is precisely because higher income groups have greater power that they can control entry so as to maintain their higher incomes. To suggest that it might be possible to introduce legislation to alter the status quo is to imply that such groups do not control the legislative process. Obviously this presents a fundamental political dilemma.

However, the crowding model suggests that the distribution of power may be critically dependent upon misinformation about the causes of inequality. The model emphasises the way in which restrictions produce differences in productivities in the long run with the result that apparently more able individuals receive higher incomes. The perpetuation of the inequality may be dependent on this kind of rationalization. It is generally accepted that inequality is largely apolitical in origin and it is on this premise that the modern theory of taxation is built. A theory of taxation which recognises institutional restrictions might provide a better understanding of the causes of inequality and so encourage consideration of more effective redistributional policies. Emphasis on institutional inequality might lead to support for legislation prohibiting restrictive practices and, as well, support to make such legislation effective.

The circularity of production functions in the crowding theory has a particular implication in respect of family policy. If circularity of production is not identified the theory of crowding reduces to a theory of non-competing labour groups as in Cairnes (1874) and recent contributions to the literature on labour market segmentation. The same concept is described in Marshall where he writes:

Let us now drop the supposition that labour is so mobile as to ensure equal remuneration for equal efforts, throughout the whole of society, and let us approach much nearer to the actual condition of life by supposing that labour is not all of one industrial grade, but of several. Let us suppose that parents always bring up their children to an occupation in their own grade; that they have a free choice within that grade, but not outside it. Lastly, let us suppose that the increase of numbers in each grade is governed by other than economic causes: as before it may be fixed, or it may be influenced by changes in custom, in moral opinion, etc. In this case also the aggregate national dividend will be governed by the abundance of nature's return to man's work in the existing state of the arts of production; but the distribution of that dividend between the different grades will be unequal [1890: VI, I f.7.pp. 513–14].

Because of circular production, the 'non-competing' labour groups develop different abilities. In modern economies with crowding inequality and a family system of access to income for children, innately identical children develop different abilities. On entry into the market sector their induced ability differences are used to justify the exclusion of some from the high wage occupations on what appear to be apolitical grounds.

The theory thus points to two paradigms crucial for the perpetuation of inequality: (a) the belief that income differences are due to innate individual characteristics and (b) the acceptance of a family system of access to income for children. Since they are interdependent, it is proposed that a policy to remove the dependency of children upon the circumstances of their parents would, if effective, lead to greater equality and efficiency in the longer term than conventional income tax-transfer schemes.

The policy considered is an age tax-transfer scheme. When there already exists a social security tax and transfer scheme for retirement, the policy involves the extension of that scheme by substantial transfers to children. The transfers may be made in-kind or in cash depending on which minimises intra-family and, in turn, inter-family shifting of benefits. In terms of intergenerational trade, an age tax-transfer scheme takes intergenerational trade outside the family. To the extent that it is effective, the trading position of the children of low income families would become more equal with that of the children of high income families. If the scheme improves the capital market by reducing the dependency of children upon parents, children emerge from stage A of the life cycle with more equal abilities. Institutional restrictions on entry into jobs are not affected directly but if the restrictions became more easily observable because differences between children are reduced, those disadvantaged might oppose the power of crowding sectors upon which restricted entry and inequality depend. The long term effectiveness of transfers providing more equal opportunities for child care and education depends upon the impact of making institutional inequality more easily observable. If low incomes and unemployment are accepted because entry into jobs is disguised as selection according to ability, or as the effect of technological constraints, inequality may no longer be acceptable when the role of the institutions is made more apparent.

The analysis of family policy identifies the diametrically opposed purposes of transfers to children and of benefits for dependent spouses. Under a joint income tax, benefits are conditional upon one spouse being dependent. Joint income taxation can increase inequality among families and between men and women even under conventional assumptions about the causes of inequality. Under institutional constraints joint taxation reinforces crowding inequality. The analysis thus points to two important directions for family policy: a change from joint income taxation to a true individual basis of tax, and the introduction of substantial transfers to children, particularly for those under school age.

8.3 Concluding comment

Progressive income tax-transfer schemes, so frequently advocated as universal solutions to problems of inequality and poverty, can be justified only if inequality is due solely to differences in innate endowments and tastes. When inequality is caused by institutional restrictions, different policy measures are required. Negative income taxation or guaranteed minimum income schemes are not solutions. Institutional inequality is the result of diverse constraints, and to determine solutions to different problems it is necessary to specify the constraints relevant to each problem.

Since policies have different effects depending upon the cause of inequality, empirical studies of the distribution of income and wealth and estimates of supply and demand elasticities can contribute to an understanding of problems and policies only if interpreted within the context of a realistic theory of the causes of inequality. Observation suggests that the theory that inequality is due solely to differences in given characteristics can only be a special case. As Adam Smith observed:

The difference of natural talents in different men is, in reality, much less than we are aware of; and the very different genius which appears to distinguish men of different professions, when grown up to maturity, is not upon many occasions so much the cause as the effect of the division of labour. The difference between the most dissimilar characters, between a philosopher and a common street porter, for example, seems to arise not so much from nature as from habit, custom, and education. When they came into the world ... they were perhaps very much alike, ... soon after they came to be employed in very different occupations. The difference of talents comes then to be taken notice of, and widens by degrees, till at last the vanity of the philosopher is willing to acknowledge scarce any resemblance [1776: p. 120].

Notes

1 Introduction: The theory in outline

1. Optimal tax theory is an application of the general theory of second best (see Lipsey and Lancaster (1956–7)) to tax design when there are one or more additional constraints, such as the untaxability of leisure.
2. See Johnson and Mieszkowski (1970) and Jones (1971a). A review of applications of the Harberger model can be found in McLure (1975) and of the literature on distortions and differentials in factor payments in Magee (1973).
3. Where individuals are grouped into households the results derived are relevant to individuals and hold for households only under restrictive conditions. See Apps and Jones (1980).
4. Savage (1980) examines the implicit assumptions of these models in the context of the theory of exhaustible resources and circular production.
5. See, for example, the three factor model in Jones (1971b).
6. A description of the general problem of taxing individuals in terms of taxing given characteristics is found in Atkinson and Stiglitz (1976) which draws together contributions to the theory of optimal taxation.
7. For a discussion of this point see Atkinson (1973).
8. For a collection of contributions to this topic, see von Furstenberg, Horowitz and Harrison (1974).
9. In addition to institutional conditions ('the sociology of wage determination') Thurow attributes constraints on the demand for labour to training and technological characteristics of jobs. The theory to be presented here attempts to explain differences in training and technological requirements as the effects of institutional restrictions.
10. Contributions to the public choice literature recognise interrelationships between the distribution of income and the political process. Aumann and Kurz (1977, 1978) examine relationships between tax policies and a democratic power structure. Individual characteristics such as endowments and attitudes towards risk are taken as given. The institutional theory of inequality to be developed here is concerned to explain observed differ-

113

ences in endowments and choices in terms of constraints imposed by formal and informal social institutions.

11. This premise is not meant to imply that all individuals are necessarily innately homogeneous. The object is to emphasise the importance of identifying institutional restrictions causing differences in productivities. Clearly there will always be a residual of unexplained differences. The present analysis seeks to avoid arbitrarily attributing such differences to innate abilities or tastes, for doing so begs the question as to the origin of the differences without advancing our understanding of them.

12. See Tiebout (1956), McGuire (1972, 1974) and Stiglitz (1977).

13. Such an event implies the failure of at least one contingent market which does not, per se, cause long term inequality. It is the use of power derived from the event which does.

14. This implies that the equilibrium wage for physical strength is higher than the wage for skills in which males and females are equally endowed, such as intelligence. This could only arise from the non-existence of a full set of contingent markets which implies restricted entry to the rents from the scarce natural resource, physical strength. Clearly, in modern economies no such wage advantage exists, but inequality in power does. In citing this example it is not implied here that a *wage* advantage for physical strength was, in fact, the initial cause of the inequality.

15. Different occupations and different job positions are treated as sectors in the model. Thus, the terms 'sectors', 'occupations', 'employments' and 'activities' are used interchangeably.

16. The term crowding is used by Bergmann (1971). The concept is attributed by Bergmann to Edgeworth's (1922) article on sex differences in wages. It is interesting to note that while the subject of Edgeworth's paper is the wage effects of restricting female labour to certain market occupations, he nevertheless states his own view that even in the absence of such restrictions, market wages for male and female labour would be unequal. He thus attributes unobserved and unexplained wage differentials to differences in the given characteristics of the sexes.

17. The property is specified by von Neumann as: 'Goods are produced not only from natural 'factors of production' but in the first place from each other. These processes of production may be circular, i.e. good G_1 is produced with the aid of good G_2 and G_2 with the aid of G_1' (p. 1).

18. Rawls (1971).

19. Both economies possess capital. An obvious form of capital in the hunting economy is hunting skills. A description of a grain economy in Bliss (1975, p. 4) provides another example of this kind of capital accumulation.

20. It is interesting to observe that Walras (1874) criticised Adam Smith's labour theory of value for his nation of hunters, arguing that: 'Value, thus comes from scarcity. Things other than labour, provided they are scarce, have value and are exchangeable just like labour itself. So the theory which traces the origin of value to labour is a theory that is devoid of

meaning rather than too narrow, an assertion that is gratuitous rather than unacceptable' (1954, p. 202). But a theory which allows inequality and attributes value to scarcity, without an explicit account of what is restricting entry and causing inequality, is not useful when institutional and non-institutional constraints can be shown to have opposite policy implications.

2 A theory of crowding

1. A taste for discrimination is analogous to a local public good.
2. Becker (1965) refers to 'full income' as the income an individual could spend on goods if the individual had no leisure. In other words, full income is the wage income an individual would receive by producing only for trade. In the Haig-Simons comprehensive definition of income, 'the market [trade] value of rights exercised in consumption' can be interpreted as full income. The accepted exclusion of leisure reflects the mis-specification of work and leisure.
3. If a model assumes a homogeneous population and constant returns to scale, job specialization and trade within an economy would have developed only because of scale economies which are exhausted. In other words, the existence of a local public good is required to explain the formation of a trading group or 'local community' by a homogeneous population within a country.
4. For a recent discussion of competitive equilibrium in a private ownership economy, see Dasgupta and Heal (1979).
5. See Savage (1980).
6. If there was already a division of labour because of scale economies, it would be necessary only to control the employment of factors in each sector.
7. Another way to increase demand is by misinformation about the need for a service, such as the need for medical tests and treatment.
8. Some implications of a model of this type are noted in Chapter 6.
9. Subscripts denote derivatives throughout.
10. In the example illustrated in Figure 2.1, the maximum profit per individual attainable in sector 1 is approached as the size of the group 1, and therefore the output of sector 1, approaches zero with all labour employed in sector 2.
11. At the new equilibrium we have the Cairnes (1874) non-competing labour group model in which wage differentials are determined by the demand for the product of each labour group. For a discussion of this point see Magee (1976), p. 11.
12. For a derivation of the result using the trade relation see Aitchison (forthcoming).
13. Differentiating the budget constraints in (2.7) and (2.8) with respect to p and summing over all individuals we obtain

$$x_p^1 + \gamma x_p^2 + \bar{x} x_{px}^1 + \tfrac{1}{p}(y_p^1 + \bar{x} y_{p\bar{x}}^1 + \gamma y_p^2) = 0$$

and thus

$$x_p^1 + \gamma x_p^2 + \bar{x} x_{p\bar{x}}^1 < 0$$

for

$$y_p^1 + \bar{x} y_{px}^1 + \gamma y_p^2 > 0$$

14. To show that $\dfrac{\partial x}{\partial p} > 0$, $\dfrac{\partial y}{\partial p} < 0$ under the production conditions specified, the production functions in (2.3) and (2.4) can be written as

$$k^1 = k^1(x - y^1/p, \; y^1)$$
$$k^2 = k^2(x^2, \; y - px^2)$$

Differentiating with respect to p and solving for $\dfrac{\partial x}{\partial p}$ and $\dfrac{\partial y}{\partial p}$ yields:

$$\frac{\partial x}{\partial p} = \frac{y^1 x_k k^1}{p^2(x - x_k k^1)} > 0$$

for $x_{kk} < 0$, $x_k > 0$ and

$$\frac{\partial y}{\partial p} = \frac{-x^2 y_k k^2}{y - y_k k^2} < 0$$

for $y_{kk} < 0$, $y_k > 0$ respectively.

15. That the denominator is negative can be checked by differentiating the budget constraints in (2.7) and (2.8) with respect to p and summing over all individuals.

3   The life cycle and institutional inequality

1. When contingent markets fail, the resulting inequality may be non-institutional. To consider the extent to which inequality may be institutional in origin, we assume a complete set of contingent markets in examining the possible effects of institutions.
2. When group formation is a method of tax avoidance, as in the case of the formation of a household by a market sector earner and a 'dependent' spouse, this implies additional constraints on tax design (see chapter 4). It does not mean that the group instead of the individual is the relevant unit of analysis.
3. It is assumed for simplicity that there are no resources that are scarce in their natural environments. Individual time is the only binding constraint. The introduction of scarce natural resources would make the analysis more complex but the basic conclusions concerning institutional inequality would remain unchanged.
4. The Samuelson (1958) model is for a 'consumption loan' economy by

which is implied an economy in which only labour skills are storable and the legal system does not permit slavery.

5. A subsequent paper, Samuelson (1975b), considers optimal social security.
6. See Becker (1976), p. 174.
7. Notice the implications of this point for the taxation of the imputed rental value of owner occupied housing. Under a direct income tax, housing is taxed at the rate at which wage income used to purchase housing is taxed. Proponents of a tax on the imputed rental value of owner occupied housing wish to see an additional tax on housing in the form of a tax on income from housing as a capital good. Such a tax is, in principle, distortionary unless it can be shown there are institutional conditions which justify it. The tax therefore has no sound economic basis per se, a point which is emphasised by Stretton (1974). If the untaxability of leisure is the only additional constraint on tax design, the standard indirect tax model derives rules for the optimal taxation of housing. Clearly there are other constraints. See Apps (1976) and Atkinson (1977b) for opposite policy conclusions based on alternative assumptions about relevant constraints.
8. See, for example, Meade (1978).
9. See Becker and Lewis (1973) and Becker and Tomes (1976).
10. The theory of screening presupposes there are ability differences between individuals and offers an explanation for wage differences for apparently equivalent labour in terms of imperfect information. Employers pay different wage rates to equivalent labour because ability cannot be observed directly and there are screening costs associated with identifying ability. Schooling in this context provides future employers with information about innate abilities. See, for example, the papers by Spence (1973), Arrow (1973) and Stiglitz (1975). An alternative interpretation of pay differentials for identical individuals is that the first stage of crowding according to the short-run model in Section 2.5 is being observed.
11. Note that both parents are employed in jobs with similar wage rates because we have not yet introduced crowding inequality on the basis of sex.
12. This interpretation of the theory of local public goods is based on the models in Stiglitz (1977) but is more general than the interpretation given in that paper.
13. Notice also that a theory of behaviour in terms of decision-making by households or by heads of households, as in Becker (1974), does not adequately explain behaviour if binding constraints on household formation are not identified, or if the institutional constraints on individual choices within the household which give rise to a 'head' of household are not specified.
14. Although the case studied is inequality between the market and household sectors, and within the market sector, a theory of crowding by institutional restrictions on group size is general and has a variety of

possible applications, particularly in the field of international trade.
15. The conditions required for a unique social optimum are defined in Dasgupta (1969) and include a fixed factor in order to ensure decreasing returns to scale.

4 Work, leisure, institutional restrictions

1. Household production theory developed from research into human capital and the value of time by Schultz (1961), Becker (1964) and others. The household production function was established by Becker (1965), Lancaster (1966) and Muth (1966). The theory extends economic analysis to include non-market activity. Applications include the analysis of decisions concerning the allocation of non-market time, marriage, divorce and fertility. For works in these areas see the Journal of Political Economy (1973, Vol. 81), Schultz (1974), Becker (1976) and the Journal of Political Economy (1976, Vol. 84).
2. See, for example, Mincer (1962), Willis (1973) and Gronau (1977). Willis specifically assumes that only the wife is productive at home.
3. See, for example, Mincer and Polacheck (1974).
4. For a discussion of endogenous technology and exhaustible inputs to production, see Savage (1980).
5. The child cannot be sold since slavery is not permitted, and the child's labour time cannot be sold under existing child labour laws. There are no tax advantages in forming firms to produce children because there is no revenue against which to offset costs of production. The consumption of market goods by children (including private sector child-care for preschoolers) is subject to income tax. Moreover children cannot consume within the firm because they cannot enter firms.
6. Low time values estimated for the female household wage also indicate the size of the differential between male and female wages. See, for example, Gronau (1973) and Jones (1977).
7. This could occur if women chose to form a cartel to obtain a 'rent' from the scarce own child identification skill.
8. For an exposition of the minimum sacrifice theory see Musgrave (1959) or Musgrave and Musgrave (1973) and for a discussion of the contribution of optimal tax theory in this context, see Atkinson (1973).
9. Notice that, with work defined as production for trade and leisure as production for consumption, a distinction between hours of work and level of effort is unnecessary. The distinction leads to the definition of wage income as the product of the hourly wage, level of effort and labour supply. Atkinson and Stiglitz (1976), for example, suggest that the problem of taxing ability may arise because effort and hours of work are unobservable. The authors point out that even if labour supply is observable, effort is not. Hence, the hourly wage is not perfectly correlated with ability. But the idea that individual levels of effort vary can be interpreted to mean that individual labour supplies to production for

trade vary. Inevitably, only traded goods and income from labour supply to the production of traded goods are observable. Utility maximization requires the individual to choose the level of effort which equates the ratio of marginal utilities of effort and of on-the-job leisure to the wage rate.

10. Boskin (1974) and Boskin and Sheshinski (forthcoming) identify the additional efficiency cost of joint taxation when secondary earners have greater wage elasticities than primary earners.
11. This assumes that utility functions satisfy the usual concavity properties.
12. An example of this bias in estimates of the average tax rates for couples when the wife works can be found in Chart 5 (p. 58) of the report on family units by the Organization for Economic Co-operation and Development (1977).
13. For a formulation of the optimal indirect tax problem when the un-taxability of household services produced for trade by a dependent spouse imposes an additional constraint, see Jones (forthcoming).
14. All utility functions are assumed to be twice differentiable and strictly concave.
15. Note that a dependent spouse's wage income is zero only if the value of the dependent spouse's marginal product is zero or if labour supply to the production of household services for the primary earner is zero.

5 Income taxation as a tax on trade

1. For an extension of the theory in this context see Aitchison (forthcoming).
2. I am indebted to Gary Aitchison for suggesting this approach to the definition of burdens.
3. This condition is obtained by substituting for $\partial x/\partial p$ and $\partial y/\partial p$ and by noting that $(y - y_k k^2) = p(x - x_k k^1)$ because all individuals have the same fixed endowment of time.
4. When an individual transfers market goods to the household sector for own use, with circular production functions the goods are used as factors in the household production of the individual's labour by the individual. Since the individual, in turn, transfers its labour to the market sector, the market goods are ultimately traded for household produced labour.
5. See Sandmo (1976) and Atkinson (1977a).
6. See, for example, Ashenfelter and Heckman (1973). Men who did not work during the sample year were omitted on the assumption they were at corner solutions.
7. See Hall (1973).
8. Joint taxation in this context is examined further in section 7.3.

6 Progressive income tax under institutional inequality

1. In an economy with crowding inequality we would expect to observe a correlation between school grades and type of employment when entry into a high wage occupation is on the basis of school grades. However,

school grades may only reflect induced ability differences. Thus it cannot be inferred that a correlation between wage and type of occupation reflects non-uniform differences in abilities, with higher wages for those occupations employing innate skills in scarce supply.

2. With circular production functions, the notion of innate ability differences implies a binding restriction on entry into the production of labour of the kind noted in section 2.1, and so there is a fundamental contradiction between conditions (iii) and (iv) listed by Mieszkowski. This contradiction is ignored in a neoclassical model by assuming non-circular production functions – factors are not goods. What the difference between factors and goods might be, is not usually considered in the tax literature, but it is interesting to note the distinction Samuelson (1953–4) makes in the factor price equalisation theorems. He allows goods as intermediate factors of production but not as 'primary' factors and states that 'the way to characterise a primary factor ... [is] by the fact that it cannot be produced or reproduced by homogeneous production functions'.

3. Notice that this implies that, using the conventional definitions of work and leisure, leisure is observable.

4. Boskin acknowledges that 'social institutions, e.g. mandatory retirement rules, child labor laws and the like, might make labour less than perfectly mobile between the home and the market' (p. 3) and also notes the preferential tax arrangements and social security provision for housewives. However, the analysis takes no account of these conditions and of other institutional restrictions controlling the allocation of labour and capital to market production and, in particular, to the highest wage occupations.

5. The estimate of capital in the household sector includes an estimate of the imputed income to owner occupied housing net of purchases and depreciation, income from rental housing, an imputed income to consumer durables and furnishings and the property tax component applicable to apartments and to personal property.

6. This distributional problem is well recognised in the cost–benefit literature (see, for example, Mishan (1971)). However, efficiency implications in the presence of binding institutional restrictions on group formation have not been noted.

7 Population growth and family policy

1. Samuelson (1975b) finds that the allocation between 'public thrift' (fully-funded social security) and 'private thrift' is a matter of indifference provided there is no private myopia. The question posed here assumes private myopia; that is, that each individual acts to maximize individual welfare without considering the consequence of all individuals acting in the same way.

2. References to parents' enjoyment of children here should not be in-

terpreted to imply that children are consumption items of parents. The principle that intra-family trade arises either from non-uniform differences in endowments or from scale economies, as discussed in Chapters 3 and 4, still holds.

3. Various institutional reasons for why children are not reared in firms were noted in note 5, Chapter 4.

4. As noted in Chapter 3, for an optimum intermediate rate of population growth (or decline) special conditions under which an intermediate rate of population growth minimizes per capita welfare cannot apply (Deardorff (1976), Samuelson (1976)).

5. The analysis in Apps and Stiglitz (1979) is a specialized extension of the trade tax model of income taxation presented in Apps (1980) and in Chapter 5 above.

6. These two labour supplies are represented separately in the household welfare function in Apps and Jones (1980). The analysis not only avoids aggregation of labour supplies across individuals but across occupations.

7. The Mirrlees (1972) analysis considers only child quantity decisions. Becker and Lewis (1973) and Becker and Tomes (1976) extend the analysis to take account of child quality decisions as well.

8. Since the revenue for the transfer is raised by a tax on adults, the future income of the child is also reduced. However, in the absence of a system of slavery or its equivalent, a change in the future income of a child does not alter the return to parents, although it may alter 'psychic benefits'.

9. Since the cost of full day-care for an under two year old is greater than for a two to five year old child, an under two year old child would receive a larger transfer. Transfers to school children would be adjusted for schooling costs incurred by the State. They would cover costs for before and after school care.

References

Aitchison, G. E. (forthcoming), *The Optimal Tariff Structure with Production Explicit*, Working Paper No. 9, Graduate School of Planning University of Sydney, Australia.

Apps, P. F. (1975), *Child Care Policy in the Production-Consumption Economy*, Victorian Council of Social Services, Australia.

(1976), Home Ownership, *The Australian Quarterly*, Vol. 48, pp. 64–75.

(1980), *Institutional Inequality and Tax Incidence*. Working Paper No. 3, Graduate School of Planning, University of Sydney, Australia.

Apps, P. F. and Jones, G. S. (1980), *Optimal Tax Design with the Wage Income of the 'Dependent' Spouse Untaxable*, Working Paper No. 4, Graduate School of Planning, University of Sydney, Australia.

Apps, P. F. and Stiglitz, J. E. (1979), *Individualism, Inequality and Taxation*, Mimeo.

Arrow, K. J. (1972), Some Mathematical Models of Race in the Labour Market, in *Racial Discrimination in Economic Life*, A. H. Pascal (ed), pp. 187–203 Lexington Books, D.C. Heath, Mass.

(1973), Higher Education as a Filter, *Journal of Public Economics*, Vol. 2, pp. 193–216.

Ashenfelter, O. and Heckman, J. (1973), Estimating Labor-Supply Functions, in *Income Maintenance and Labor Supply*, G. L. Cain and H. W. Watts (eds), pp. 265–78, Rand-McNally, Chicago.

Atkinson, A. B. (1973), How Progressive Should Income Tax Be?, in *Essays in Modern Economics*, The Proceedings of the Association of University Teachers of Economics: Aberystwyth 1972, M. Parkin and A. R. Nobay (eds), pp. 90–109, Longman Group Limited, London.

(1977a), Optimal taxation and the direct versus indirect tax controversy, *Canadian Journal of Economics*, Vol. 10, pp. 590–606.

(1977b), Housing Allowances, Income Maintenance and Income Taxation, in *The Economics of Public Services*, M. S. Feldstein and R. P. Inman (eds), pp. 3–16, Macmillan, London.

Atkinson, A. B. and Stiglitz, J. E. (1976), The Design of Tax Structure: Direct Versus Indirect Taxation, *Journal of Public Economics*, Vol. 6, pp. 55–76.

123

Aumann, R. J. and Kurz, M. (1977), Power and Taxes, *Econometrica*, Vol. 45, pp. 1137–61.

(1978), Power and Taxes in a Multi-Commodity Economy (Updated), *Journal of Public Economics*, Vol. 9, pp. 139–161.

Becker, G. S. (1957), *Economics of Discrimination*, University of Chicago Press, Chicago.

(1960), An Economic Analysis of Fertility, in *Demographic and Economic Change in Developed Countries*, Universities – National Bureau of Economic Research, Princeton, US.

(1964), *Human Capital*, National Bureau of Economic Research, New York.

(1965), A Theory of the Allocation of Time, *The Economic Journal*, Vol. 75, pp. 493–517.

(1973). A Theory of Marriage: Part 1, *Journal of Political Economy*, Vol. 81, pp. 813–46. A Theory of Marriage: Part 2, *Journal of Political Economy*, Vol. 82, pp. 1063–91.

(1974), A Theory of Social Interactions, *Journal of Political Economy*, Vol. 82, pp. 1063–91.

(1976), *The Economic Approach to Human Behavior*, University of Chicago Press, Chicago.

Becker, G. S. and Lewis, H. G. (1973), On the Interaction Between the Quality and Quantity of Children, *Journal of Political Economy*, Vol. 81, pp. S279–S288.

Becker, G. S. and Tomes, N. (1976), Child Endowments and the Quantity and Quality of Children, *Journal of Political Economy*, Vol. 84, pp. S143–S162.

Bergmann, B. R. (1971), The Effects on White Incomes of Discrimination in Employment, *Journal of Political Economy*, Vol. 79, pp. 294–313.

Bliss, C. (1975), *Capital Theory and the Distribution of Income*, North-Holland, Amsterdam.

Boskin, M. J. (1973), The Economics of Labor Supply, in *Income Maintenance and Labor Supply*, G. L. Cain and H. W. Watts (eds), pp. 163–80, Rand-McNally, Chicago.

(1974), The Effects of Government Expenditures and Taxes on Female Labor, *American Economic Review*, Vol. 64, pp. 251–6.

(1975), Efficiency Aspects of the Differential Tax Treatment of Market and Household Economic Activity, *Journal of Public Economics*, Vol. 4, pp. 1–25.

Boskin, M. J. and Sheshinski, E. (forthcoming), Optimal Tax Treatment of the Family: Married Couples, *Journal of Public Economics*.

Cairnes, J. E. (1874), *Some Leading Principles of Political Economy*, Macmillan, London.

Dasgupta, P. S. (1969), On the Concept of Optimum Population, *Review of Economic Studies*, Vol. 36, pp. 295–318.

Dasgupta, P. S. and Heal, G. M. (1979), *Economic Theory and Exhaustible Resources*, Cambridge University Press, Cambridge, UK.

Deardorff, A. V. (1976), The Growth Rate for Population: Comment, *International Economic Review*, Vol. 17, pp. 510–15.

De Tray, D. N. (1973), Child Quality and the Demand for Children, *Journal of Political Economy*, Vol. 81, pp. S70–S95.

Diamond, P. (1965), National Debt in a Neoclassical Growth Model, *American Economic Review*, Vol. 55, pp. 1126–50.

Diamond, P. and Mirrlees, J. A. (1971), Optimal Taxation and Public Production: I and II, *American Economic Review*, Vol. 61, pp. 8–27, 261–78.

Dixit, A. and Sandmo, A. (1977), Some Simplified Formulae for Optimal Income Taxation, *Scandinavian Journal of Economics*, Vol. 79, pp. 417–23.

Doeringer, P. B. and Piore, M. J. (1971), *Internal Labor Markets and Manpower Analysis*, Lexington Books, D.C. Heath, Mass.

(1975), Unemployment and the Dual Labor Market, *The Public Interest*, No. 38, pp. 67–79.

Edgeworth, F. Y. (1922), Equal Pay to Men and Women for Equal Work, *The Economic Journal*, Vol. 31, pp. 431–57.

Gronau, R. (1973), The Intrafamily Allocation of Time: The Value of Housewives' Time, *American Economic Review*, Vol. 63, pp. 634–51.

(1977), Leisure, Home Production and Work – The Theory of The Allocation of Time Revisited, *Journal of Political Economy*, Vol. 85, pp. 1099–123.

Hall, R. E. (1973), Wages, Income and Hours of Work in the U.S. Labor Force, in *Income Maintenance and Labor Supply*, G. L. Cain and H. W. Watts (eds), pp. 102–62, Rand-McNally, Chicago.

Harberger, A. C. (1962), The Incidence of the Corporation Tax, *Journal of Political Economy*, Vol. 70, pp. 215–40.

Harrison, A. J. and Quarmby, D. A. (1972), The Value of Time, in *Cost Benefit Analysis*, R. Layard (ed), pp. 173–208, Penguin Books, Harmondsworth, UK.

Johnson, H. G. and Mieszkowski, P. (1970), The Effects of Unionization on the Distribution of Income: A General Equilibrium Approach, *Quarterly Journal of Economics*, Vol. 84, pp. 539–61.

Jones, G. S. (1977), Labour Mobility, Time Values, and Technology in Domestic Production, *Environment and Planning B.*, Vol. 4, pp. 99–113.

(forthcoming), *Optimal Commodity Taxation with Household Services Produced by a Dependent Spouse Untaxable*. Working Paper No. 5, Graduate School of Planning, University of Sydney, Australia.

Jones, G. S. and Savage, E. J. (forthcoming), *Optimal Taxation with Intra-sector Wage Incomes and Leisure Untaxable*. Working Paper No. 6, Graduate School of Planning, University of Sydney, Australia.

Jones, W. J. (1971a), Distortions in Factor Markets and the General Equilibrium Model of Production, *Journal of Political Economy*, Vol. 79, pp. 437–59.

(1971b), A Three-Factor Model in Theory, Trade, and History, in

Trade, Balance of Payments and Growth, J. N. Bhagwati, R. W. Jones, R. A. Mundell and J. Vanek (eds), pp. 3–21, North-Holland, Amsterdam.

Lancaster, K. J. (1966), A New Approach to Consumer Theory, *Journal of Political Economy*, Vol. 74, pp. 132–57.

Lipsey, R. G. and Lancaster, K. J. (1956–7), The General Theory of Second Best, *Review of Economic Studies*, Vol. 24, pp. 11–32.

McGuire, M. C. (1972), Private Good Clubs and Public Good Clubs: Economic Models of Group Formation, *Swedish Journal of Economics*, Vol. 74, pp. 84–99.

(1974), Group Segregation and Optimal Jurisdictions, *Journal of Political Economy*, Vol. 82, pp. 112–32.

McLure, C. E. (1975), General Equilibrium Incidence Analysis, *Journal of Public Economics*, Vol. 4, pp. 125–61.

Magee, S. P. (1973), Factor Market Distortions, Production and Trade: A Survey, *Oxford Economic Papers*, Vol. 25, pp. 1–43.

(1976), *International Trade and Distortions in Factor Markets*, New York.

Marshall, A. (1890), *Principles of Economics*, Vol. 6, Macmillan, London.

Meade, J. E. (1955), *The Theory of International Economic Policy, Vol. II: Trade and Welfare*, Oxford University Press.

Meade, J. E. et al. (1978), *The Structure and Reform of Direct Taxation*, Institute of Fiscal Studies, Allen and Unwin, London.

Mieszkowski, P. (1969), Tax Incidence Theory: The Effects of Taxes on Distribution of Income, *Journal of Economic Literature*, Vol. 7, pp. 1103–24.

Mincer, J. (1962), Labor Force Participation of Married Women, in *Aspects of Labor Economics*, H. G. Lewis (ed), pp. 63–105, Universities National Bureau of Economic Research, Princeton, NJ, Princeton University Press.

Mincer, J. and Polachek, S. (1974), Family Investments in Human Capital: Earnings of Women, *Journal of Political Economy*, Vol. 88, pp. S76–S108.

Mirrlees, J. A. (1971), An Exploration in the Theory of Optimum Income Taxation, *Review of Economic Studies*, Vol. 38, pp. 175–208.

(1972), Population Policy and the Taxation of Family Size, *Journal of Public Economics*, Vol. 1, pp. 169–98.

Mishan, E. J. (1971), *Cost-Benefit Analysis*, George Allen and Unwin, London.

Musgrave, R. A. (1959), *The Theory of Public Finance*, McGraw-Hill, New York.

Musgrave, R. A. and Musgrave, P. B. (1973), *Public Finance in Theory and Practice*, McGraw-Hill, New York.

Muth, R. (1966), Household Production and Consumer Demand Functions, *Econometrica*, Vol. 34, pp. 699–708.

Neher, P. A. (1971), Peasants, Procreation and Pensions, *American Economic Review*, Vol. 61, pp. 380–89.

Organization for Economic Co-operation and Development, (1977), *The Treatment of Family Units in OECD Member Countries under Tax and Transfer Systems*, A Report by the Committee on Fiscal Affairs, Paris.

Pigou, A. C. (1922), *A Study in Public Finance*, Macmillan and Co., London.

Ramsey, F. F. (1927), A Contribution to the Theory of Taxation, *Economic Journal*, Vol. 37, pp. 47–61.

Razin, A. and Ben-Zion, U. (1975), An Intergenerational Model of Population Growth, *American Economic Review*, Vol. 65, pp. 923–34.

Rawls, J. (1971), *A Theory of Justice*, Harvard University Press, Cambridge, Mass.

Samuelson, P. A. (1953–4), Prices of Factors and Goods in General Equilibrium, *Review of Economic Studies*, Vol. 21, pp. 1–20.

(1958), An Exact Consumption-Loan Model of Interest with or without the Social Contrivance of Money, *Journal of Political Economy*, Vol. 66, pp. 467–82.

(1968), The Two-Part Golden Rule Deduced as the Asymptotic Turnpike of Cartinary Motions, *Western Economic Journal*, Vol. 6, pp. 85–89.

(1975a), The Optimum Growth Rate for Population, *International Economic Review*, Vol. 16, pp. 531–38.

(1975b), Optimum Social Security in a Life-Cycle Growth Model, *International Economic Review*, Vol. 16, pp. 539–44.

(1976), The Optimum Growth Rate for Population: Agreement and Evaluations, *International Economic Review*, Vol. 17, pp. 539–44.

Sandmo, A. (1976), Optimal Taxation, *Journal of Public Economics*, Vol. 6, pp. 37–54.

Savage, E. J. (1980), *Exhaustible Resources, Capital and Time: Implications for General Equilibrium Taxation*, Working Paper No. 2, Graduate School of Planning, University of Sydney, Australia.

Schultz, T. W. (1961), Investment in Human Capital, *American Economic Review*, Vol. 51, pp. 1–17, reprinted in *Economics of Education* 1, M. Blaug (ed) (1968), Penguin Modern Economics, Penguin Books.

(ed) (1974), *Economics of the Family: Marriage, Children and Human Capital*, a conference of the National Bureau of Economic Research, University of Chicago Press, Chicago and London.

Sheshinski, E. (1972), The Optimal Linear Income Tax, *Review of Economic Studies*, Vol. 39, pp. 297–302.

Simons, H. C. (1938), *Personal Income Taxation*, University of Chicago Press, Chicago.

Smith, A. (1776), *The Wealth of Nations*, A Skinner (ed) (1974), Pelican Classics, Penguin Books Ltd., U.K.

Spence, M. (1973), Job Market Signaling, *Quarterly Journal of Economics*, Vol. 87, pp. 355–79.

Stiglitz, J. E. (1975), The Theory of 'Screening', Education and the Distribution of Income, *American Economic Review*, Vol. 65, pp. 283–300.

(1977), The Theory of Local Goods, in *The Economics of Public Services*, M. S. Feldstein and R. P. Inman (eds), pp. 274–333, Macmillan, London.

Stretton, H. (1974), *Housing and Government*, Boyer Lectures, Australian Broadcasting Commission, Sydney.

Tiebout, C. M. (1956), A Pure Theory of Local Public Expenditures, *Journal of Public Economics*, Vol. 69, pp. 416–24.

Thurow, L. C. (1972), Education and Economic Equality, *The Public Interest*, No. 28, pp. 66–81.

(1975), *Generating Inequality, Mechanisms of Distribution in the U.S. Economy*, Basic Books Inc., N.Y.

von Furstenberg, G. M. Horowitz, A. R. and Harrison, B. (eds) (1974), *Patterns of Racial Discrimination, Vol. II: Employment and Income*, Lexington Books, D.C. Heath, Mass.

von Neumann, J. (1945), A Model of General Equilibrium, *Review of Economic Studies*, Vol. 13, pp. 1–9.

Walras, L. (1874), *Elements d'Economie Politique Pure*, Lausanne. Translation by William Jaffe, 1954, George Allen and Unwin Ltd. U.K.

Willis, R. J. (1973), A New Approach to the Economic Theory of Fertility Behavior, *Journal of Political Economy*, Vol. 81, pp. S14–S64.

Index